Jumping Ship

How to Keep Your Children from Jumping Ship

by Michael Pearl

Jumping Ship ®
Copyright © 2007 by Michael Pearl
ISBN-13: 978-1-892112-98-9

TABLE OF CONTENTS

JUMPING SHIP

CHAPTER 1

JUMPING SHIP

The homeschool movement has matured to the point that we now have a large pool of graduates from which to survey our successes and failures, and, if need be, to modify our course accordingly. The first wave, in their late twenties to early thirties, are now married and have children of their own. There are many success stories among them. Their successes can be measured by the many attorneys, doctors, scientists, teachers, and statesmen who are now making a difference in the world and in the lives of the individuals they touch. But it is best measured by the emotional stability and spiritual perspective that homeschooled young people have carried into their marriages.

Regardless of the prestige of their vocations, we now have a new generation of godly parents that were not suckled by the world. They are building heavenly marriages and raising a fresh new breed of stable, godly children. While the public school system continues to degenerate into a drug-stupid, sex-oriented, illiterate morass of misfit Marxist clones, the homeschool movement is producing intelligent, clear-thinking, confident citizens ready to stand in the middle of the cascading corruption and declare their allegiance to God and family.

However, not all homeschoolers become success stories. A few fail to measure up fully, while a small percentage fail miserably. Not all homeschool families are created equally, because homeschool children are the direct product of the culture their parents provide them. There is nothing magical about homeschooling itself. It is just a context in which to conduct parenting without interference from humanistic government and the influence of a growing variety of contemporary cultures, all of which are causing the "devil-lution" of society. When parents choose to homeschool, they are choosing to become the primary example and the prevailing culture for their children. They are "cloning" their worldview—a most sobering venture.

However, there are failures, and they can be traced to two primary problems. In the first place, some parents are not good stock for "cloning." That is, not even the world wants or needs more people "just like them." Secondly, and this will be the main point of our present discussion, there is nothing easy or automatic about culture cloning. You cannot take for granted that your children are going to adopt your perspective on life. It takes serious commitment and wisdom to duplicate your heart and soul in your children.

There was a time, many years ago, when community life (church, school, the extended family, friends and neighbors) all pointed children in the right direction, a godly direction. Sometimes, when parents failed to be good trainers and examples, their deficiency was rectified by grandparents, aunts, uncles, cousins, the government school, and the local church, around which all social life revolved. But no more. The average church today will send your children to hell as fast as the local DVD rental store. Community life has gone the way of the old familiar front porch and grandma sitting there shelling beans. Today, you even have to be on guard with your uncles and cousins, who may attempt to molest your children. Our present culture is scary enough to send a family packing to the Amazon, taking their chances with drug lords, anacondas, malaria, and socialist dictators.

We are receiving far too many letters from parents who tell us that their older children, 15 to 18 years old, are jumping ship, bailing out, changing sides, or looking for the meaning of life on the other side of the tracks. Parents are shocked. They tell us, "I kept them from the TV. We homeschooled and homechurched, were careful to only associate with families of like mind. We taught them the Word of God and protected them from evil influences; but the first chance they got to join the world's parade, they did so without hesitation." One woman wrote and told us that she discovered that her two teenage homeschooled boys had been engaging in sodomy since before they went through puberty. Another family discovered that all eight of their children were engaging in group incest, in the first degree. Children everywhere are finding ways to access pornography on the web. One kid was slipping into his neighbor's house to view it on their computer when they were gone. A sixteen-year-old girl ran away and shacked up with a druggie. In two years, she was a drunk and a drug addict with a child and a broken jaw, from when her shiftless man busted her one for sassing him. When one family discovered that their children were engaged in incest, the mother and father stopped going to church and took up drinking. The whole family went to hell with an "I don't care" attitude. Later, one of the girls, now grown, wrote to us to decry their shameful condition. She told how the family had done devotionals every day and did not watch TV. They did all the "right things", but "it just did not take" with the kids. She got saved after getting married and having three children, and then became concerned for the rest of her family, especially her lesbian sister.

I know this is depressing to you, because it has depressed me to write it. But you need to be forewarned in order to be armed for the spiritual battle for your children's souls. So the question I seek to answer is, "What can I do to ensure that my children do not jump ship when they get to be 16 or 18 years old?" Let me reframe the question a few times, and then see if you catch a hint of what the answer will be.

- What can I do to be sure that my children are actually embracing the values that we teach?
- What can I do to prepare my children to resist the temptations of the world?
- How can I impart a knowledge of good and evil to my children that will cause them to choose the good?
- How can I forewarn and forearm my children without taking away their innocence?
- How can I cause them to love righteousness and hate iniquity?
- How can I cause them to be patient and wait for the spouse God has prepared for them?

It is hard for me to communicate with many of you, because you have been blinded by "religion". Even now as you read this, you likely think I am talking about someone else. You are confident that your family is secure in Bible principles and religious devotion. You have given them a "packaged Christianity" and isolated them from any outside influences, and you are confident that they are safe behind the fence.

There are two problem areas that you should consider. The first one is your own negative example. I realize that you are tired of my being negative about this critical issue. You want to hear something positive, and you want an easy fix. I know from 50 years of reflective experience that we sons of Adam want the peaceable fruits of righteousness, but we want it in a system that can be applied externally without intruding into our personal sanctum. When things go bad at work, we reorganize, take a different approach, have some motivational meetings, discover some missing secrets that will revolutionize production. We may have to admit that we were ignorant of some things and that there is a better way, and we will have to make some changes; this we can live with and not feel diminished in our ego. But to admit that deep down in our souls we are ugly, cruel, selfish, mean, indifferent, caught up in vanities, lustful and, in general, just a lousy person who is not fit to be anyone's friend, mush less a parent, is a repentance few parents are willing to confess.

We want a do-it-yourself remake of our ailing family that leaves our own private souls alone. In other words, we don't want our whole life fixed, just the visible problems in the lives of our children. We don't want to be bothered by anything except the poor state of the kids. If we can fix them, we can live with the rest of the status quo. But such thinking will never work, because we are a *whole* person. You cannot be a good father without being a good husband or wife. You cannot be a good father without being a person of discipline and self-control. You cannot be a good example to your children without being a good example to everyone who knows you. Good Christian fathers and mothers are only made from good Christians. You can't be right in one area while being wrong in others. We are a whole person and must understand that any child-training "fix" must involve the whole person. In short, I am calling you—the whole person—to personal repentance. The "fix" will come soon afterwards.

You must *be* all that you want your children to be. You can't drive or drag teenagers to godliness and heaven; you must lead them. That will be the first point of our discussion. Secondly, you must not assume that innocence is a hedge. The enemy is not always on the "outside" of your home. There is a big enough and bad enough enemy within the flesh of your own children to scare an angel to death. A child who never even heard of sex of any kind, never saw an example, never has been tempted by any outside source, can discover it on his own and then end up engaging in incest. Genuinely good parents who actually provide righteous examples can have their children descend into debauchery right in the middle of their carefully constructed and properly maintained sanctuary. While a father and mother are standing guard at the gate that leads out into the world, children of Adam's descent can build their own Sodom from scratch, right under the best example that loving, careful, attentive parents can provide.

There is an answer which we will soon come to, but please know that it is not to be found in performing the externals of Christianity. You cannot focus your energies on building walls against the darkness outside the home. You must build walls within that admit lots of heavenly sunlight.

ABOVE ALL

For starters, you must sell your children on your worldview. It must be an active, attractive and convincing presentation, for you are not the only salesman calling on your children. They must be personally convinced that the worldview you recommend and exemplify is the best of all possible alternatives. They will not be fooled with pretense. By the time a kid is sixteen years old, he will know you better than you know yourself. Teenagers are forming their values based on what they see as valuable. No one can constrain another person to adopt certain values. Generally, everyone values what promises to fulfill his deepest desires. If the thing you offer your children does not appeal to them, they will reject it, as they should. Why would anyone choose a path that appears to lead to misery, boredom, or loneliness? How can someone value what is of no value? Teenagers want romance and passion. Girls want tenderness and security with their passion. Boys want a challenge in which to be engaged in conquest. Everyone needs a vision and the means to fulfill it. The quest for goodness and productivity is not enough to contain a sixteen-year-old. Duty and respectability will likely not be their controlling drives.

Many families operate by a tradition of being "good Christian people." They are hard-working, honest, and respectable. They choose to live a "good life" and avoid the consequences of sin, so they naturally expect their children to see the wisdom of this lifestyle and choose it for themselves. Their good lifestyle is the product of their religious convictions, and they fully expect that their children will see that. They couldn't even imagine that their children might choose the obviously less fulfilling, low-class life of shameful sin.

Parents make the mistake of thinking that their "good life" is automatically a recommendation for the Christian life, but a "good life" can be lived by anyone of any religion, or by an atheist, for that matter, as observation so easily attests. There are Sodomites in the public schools who are happier than some Christians. There are fornicators and adulterers who love each other more than some Christian parents love each other. The movies represent evil people as full of life and fun. Video games, bursting with big-busted women and powerful young men slaying their adversaries, become substitutes for the boys' need of conquest, and suggest an approach to life that is hedonistic. A trip to the mall reveals to the young person that there is a lot of "loving fun" over on the other side. What have you got that is better? How do they know it to be so? Children come into the world with no knowledge of good and evil. Parents think that if they keep them from knowing evil, then good will be the default position. But did not Adam and Eve, surrounded with only good, choose the evil? There are no second generation Christians. Each child invents his own life according to his perception of what satisfies.

There are actually only two kinds of lives lived on this planet. The "natural life", whether in doing evil or doing good, or somewhere in between, and the "Jesus life," which is infinitely more than a life of doing or being good. Jesus said, "I am come that they might have life, and that they might have it more abundantly" (John 10:10). The Jesus life is an abundant life of joy and love. It is a life of honesty, judgment, and sacrificial service. There is no hypocrisy in the Jesus life. "But the fruit of the Spirit is love, joy, peace, longsuffering, gentleness, goodness, faith, meekness, temperance..." (Galatians 5:22-23). Peter says, "ye rejoice with joy unspeakable and full of glory..." (1 Peter 1:8). Do your children know you as a person who rejoices with "joy unspeakable", and do they see your life as being "full of glory"? Then, what do you have to offer your kids that will hold them to your worldview? How is the life you have chosen better than any other? Prove it to them without joy, and you will have done the preposterous.

A "good" life without any passion is not worth repeating. Love is always passionate. So is joy and peace. Longsuffering is passionate in its quiet reserve, taking into consideration the needs and feelings of others. Gentleness and goodness are virtues that point to God like a big red arrow. Faith is as lovely as a cherub's wings. Meekness never allows others to feel inferior, and temperance is the ultimate demonstration of the power of God in one's life. The fruit of the Spirit is attractive, indeed! Teenagers are attracted to attractive people. If their parents are unattractive, they will fix their admiring gaze on someone who is attractive. A light-hearted spirit of joy and praise is attractive to everyone. Religious convictions worn only on the shirtsleeves are about as attractive as a man sneezing in your face.

The problem is that teenagers are not wise in discerning the difference between true joy and cheap laughter. But, they can easily discern when their parents don't have any joy at all. And then they come across a person of the world who is light-hearted and full of fun. What do you expect them to do? They don't see the cynicism and rebellion behind the feigned joy. They just know that for the first time in their short lives, they have found a context for their passion. When they are with those kinds of people, they feel alive. They suddenly have hope that life is not always going to be dull and boring.

They find unconditional acceptance with the people of darkness, and since they have never really experienced God's love in the natural context of their home, they think this is the love they have always missed. They will walk away from their dull parents and right into the Devil's den without any doubt that they have finally found true meaning in life. They are indeed fools, but their parents were foolishly naïve enough to believe that their teenagers would be content to accept the middle-of-the-road, principled but passionless religion that never brought a fountain of joy.

Parents' ability to communicate their worldview to their children is mostly bound up in their personal relationship to each other. If Mother and Father have a romance that is visible, a joy that is uncontained, and a passion that is enviable, their children will want to travel the same road in hopes of reaping the same fruit in their own lives.

CHAPTER 2

FRUIT BEARING

The following is just one example of many letters we have received, relating to our topic..

Dear Pearls,

We know a family who homeschooled their children and have been used by ministries as an example of a model Christian family. Their oldest son just jumped ship. He has a wild tattoo, pierced his ears, and dyed his hair. But more than his bizarre looks, he is totally rebellious. I must admit, his jumping ship left me shaken until I read your article, and then I could see what led to his demise. His parents are fretful folks, always worried about spending money, the state of the country, or the evil influence of the neighbors or church. The last word I would ever use to describe them is joyful. Their relationship seems strained. If I were a child, I would not want to live with that family. I think that is a pretty good gauge by which to check myself.

Steve

The first crop of homeschoolers has matured; the fruit is ripe; the time of reaping has come. It is not the day of judgment, but to many parents, it feels akin to the Great Tribulation. Parents are seeing their own flesh and blood take on characteristics of the enemy. Regretfully, this is not a surprise to many of us. We have seen it coming for many years, predicted it in our writings, and warned parents that carefully constructed religious teaching and withdrawal from worldliness were not enough. The fences parents build are able to constrain children when they are young, but the time comes, around sixteen to eighteen years of age, when the kids have the power to choose and act for themselves. Every one of those parents holds their breath. It reminds me of Joel 3:14: "Multitudes, multitudes in the valley of decision: for the day of the LORD is near in the valley of decision."

Where can a family go to save its children? Escaping from the world is like escaping from your own skin. While we peer behind us, hoping to have eluded the enemy, we discover that he is standing in our shoes. Many Christian families have been very careful to protect their children, only to discover that the Devil is in the air we breathe, the food we eat, and even in the sex organs of a thirteen-year-old.

Many of these parents have had their faith shaken. "We didn't watch television or associate with sinners; we taught our children Christian principles; why didn't it work?" It is almost as though Christians are believing the leftist propaganda that environment and heredity are the factors that determine a person's behavior. Parents seem to believe that they can condition their children into being good Christians by protecting them and teaching them Christian principles. Reality has proven that old premise to be false: "Save them from corrupt influences, and they will never corrupt."

The fallen sons of Adam, in every generation, have the inherent capability and propensity to recreate sin, even in the protected vacuum of a Christian home. Children do not need to be exposed to "bad people" to do bad things. The children of Christians are not exempt from the lure of the flesh. Innocence is not a protective hedge, as we know by the example of Adam and Eve. Christian character cannot be transmitted at birth, or passed on as a family heritage. "As it is written, There is none righteous, no, not one: There is none that understandeth, there is none that seeketh after God. They are all gone out of the way, they are together become unprofitable: there is none that doeth good, no, not one. For all have sinned, and come short of the glory of God" (Romans 3:10-12, 23).

Enough! This is depressing. What of the Scripture that promises "Train up a child in the way he should go: and when he is old, he will not depart from it" (Proverbs 22:6)? It is still true and has proven so in the experience of tens of thousands of kids who have gone on to become stable, hard-working, righteous children of God who are now starting their own families and are already seeing blessed third-generation fruit.

We hear it often, "I did train them, but it did not work." The key is in the word "train." Not just any training will do. The *effort* put into training is not the same as *actual* training.

A PARABLE: THE FAMILY CRUISE

Every family is a ship with a captain, a crew, and sometimes passengers and cargo. It may be a pleasure liner, a research vessel, a boatload of pilgrims headed to a new city, a mercy ship, a cargo vessel seeking riches, or a stinking old tub hanging around port. There are many ships leaving port, each with a purpose and destination: all on board are participants, regardless of the degree of their commitment, and their lives are affected by the passage and the destination. No ship is alone. Others are always sailing nearby, and the crew becomes acquainted with many ships and their crews. In each port, there is a mingling and exchange of news and gossip. Every crew member is always weighing the possibilities and deciding if he is on the best ship.

No ship is an island unto itself. If a captain were to simply anchor offshore to avoid the corruption of society and to prevent his crew members from being tempted to switch ships, the hands would become very discontent. *The ship must be going somewhere with a meaningful purpose, otherwise the crew would not long tolerate the drudgery of their daily duties.* There is no romance in simply retreating, or in seeking one's own survival. The thrill of life is in the conquest of the obstacles of life.

Many fathers/captains are afraid of failure, so they go nowhere and do nothing but seek to stay afloat just outside the influence of other ships. The crew of a self-quarantined ship will stand at the rail and longingly watch other ships sail past to destinations unknown. They know that those ships that are going someplace, any place, must certainly be more interesting than the stagnant calm in which they must exist. Younger kids will wish for something different, but fear and insecurity will keep them at the rail. However, there will come a day when they think they can swim well enough to risk going overboard to catch a ride on a passing vessel.

What will keep kids from jumping ship and booking passage to a different port is the confidence that their ship is going somewhere, sailing to a port that offers tremendous possibilities. They should be able to stand on the bow and imagine the great new world to which they are sailing. They must have an exciting vision of great things to come and a hope of being significant in those coming events.

They must have obtained a sense of mission, a full understanding of the history of their captain's and ship's endeavor. They should be familiar with those who have gone before and should be made aware that they are needed to carry on the worthy tradition. Only then will they endure the hardships of the voyage without crumbling under the burden of daily, monotonous routine.

They must feel that their part in the voyage is primarily a means of service to others, and that the boat and those on it are not the final end. Without the moral compass that comes from dedicating one's life to service, they cannot develop great courage and fortitude. The sense of moral rightness that comes from serving others is a driving force that will not accept defeat. It imparts courage and unrelenting perseverance.

The ship must be provisioned with entertainment, although the crew will not be satisfied simply being entertained passengers. The very essence of the ship must lie in its purpose, a mission beyond a simple pleasure cruise. They will not be satisfied with being little more than cargo. Being a vital crew member and knowing it, in the mind of children, is the seed that will later blossom into the revolutionary thought: Someday, I will be a captain, with a ship of my own.

Yes, they must, from the youngest age, be learning to pilot the ship. And, they should be made to know that they are in training to become a captain of their own ship and that they can be trusted with real responsibility.

They must taste of the glory and the triumph from time to time. Keeping them on the edge of expectancy will be an integral part of *keeping them!*

There must be authority on the ship that provides security and promotes admiration. There is nothing more emotionally dissatisfying to young people than disorganization and lack of a top commander who is decisive, resolute, even hard and unyielding at times. The ship must have one authority that is respected. If the chief officer is subversive and disrespectful, it will cause the crew to commit mutiny or to abandon ship in some promising port.

It should be common knowledge among the crew that the ship, although seeming to be sailing alone most of the time, is part of a large armada, all traveling to the same location for the same great purpose. The ship and its crew should be in contact with other ships of the line who share the same destination. The crew should never be left with a feeling of isolation.

Every person on board must know that the captain is answerable to a higher commander who holds the power of life and death. The crew must be caused to fear the higher powers, including their captain.

The captain must conduct himself with dignity, integrity, and honor if he is to maintain the respect of his crew. Yet, he must always be approachable, accessible, and willing to work harder and serve more diligently than they all.

The captain must be willing to mete out discipline when it is called for, never vacillating, and never being squeamish in his role as commander.

Weathering storms together and overcoming adversity are not things to decry, for they will create a bond of mutual respect between the officers and the crew.

It is a fundamental necessity that the ship be maintained in such a manner that every person on board takes responsibility for and pride in his ship.

SAILING WITH A PURPOSE

Now let's give closer attention to the first three paragraphs in our parable. The third paragraph sums up our present subject, which we state again.

To keep kids from jumping ship and booking passage to a different port, they must have confidence that the ship is going somewhere, to a port that offers tremendous possibilities. They should be able to stand up on the bow and imagine the new world out there to which they are sailing. They must be given an exciting vision of great things to come and a hope of being significant in those coming events.

Children are, after all, people—unfinished adults, full of untested passions and expectations. They are experiencing many new drives and pleasures. I remember when I was a child, the world into which I was growing was exciting and wonderful. I felt like a kid at one of those carnivals where admission is five dollars and you can ride everything as many times as you want. At ten years of age, I wanted to eat one whole fried chicken and two chocolate pies all by myself (in one sitting), with no one there to stop me. I wanted a girl of my own to smell and touch. I wanted a boat to sail, and a gun and all the shells I could shoot. I wanted a truck so I could go places and see wonderful things. I dreamed of painting pictures and building structures out of lumber and metal. I wanted to touch everything and own two of them.

As I got a little older and came to know the Lord as my personal savior, I developed new passions. I wanted to change the world and make everybody do right, which included wanting to convert sinners to Christ. By the time I was eighteen years old, I wanted to straighten out my parents, my church, and all my siblings. I still wanted a girl of my own to smell and touch, but by then I had decided that I also wanted one who could talk to me and listen to my ideas about changing the world. I was now down to two pieces of pie and only half of a chicken. Today, I want two pieces of chicken, and I pass up the pie. I got that girl when I was twenty-five. I still touch and smell her, and she listens to my ideas and I to hers. We talk long hours about the needs of others and what we can do to help. We have not changed the world, but we have occupied ourselves diligently in accomplishing what God had gifted us to do. Life has been richer than I could have ever imagined. From the very beginning of our lives together as parents, I tried to instill this love of life into my children.

Now, you may think that this just sounds like an old man reminiscing. Maybe so, but listen carefully to his musings, because with this line of thought I am going someplace very important. Today I took my granddaughter Laura Rose, not yet three, down to the sawmill to help debark some trees in preparation for sawing. She picked up the tool and grunted dutifully while she dug at the bark. When a slab of bark broke loose and fell away from the log, she was delighted with her power. She was helping Big Papa. She was important. She is not a passenger on a pleasure liner. She is part of the crew. When she comes into the house, Deb doesn't send her into the playroom. She is not even interested in the big box of toys that we keep for the kids. She wants to put clothes in the laundry, wash the dishes, mop the floor, fix dinner for Big Papa, or any constructive chore that Deb is doing at the time.

THIRTEEN-YEAR-OLD

I have a young man thirteen years old who comes over and works with me outdoors. Like most thirteen-year-olds, he doesn't actually crave work. He quickly tires of any job that is hard and boring, but if he is working beside me, he will do the same difficult job all day long and think he is having fun. He is a skinny, awkward boy, going through puberty and imagining all the wonderful things that await him. Just the other day he said, "I want to get me a wife." He said it without any inhibition, just as he would tell me he wanted to get a new bicycle. There was a hungry look in his eyes and an eagerness in his changing voice.

He loves my Kubota tractor, especially when operating the front-end loader. While he is doing manual work, he always keeps his eye on that tractor. And I have learned that if I let him drive it at least once every hour to go get a tool or to move a log, I can keep him doing the boring chores with enthusiasm. He loves to operate a chain saw, weed eater, or any power tool. He has also been eyeing my red truck—no, not yet! He is too uncoordinated.

You can't just use kids as a source of cheap labor. They will not be happy being nothing more than domestic servants onboard your ship. You must, from time to time, with some supervision, let them do the navigation and pilot the ship. I keep the kids in my charge on the cutting edge of experience, never allowing things to stay boring for long. If we are moving sawdust and I make this young man do the shoveling but don't allow him to drive the tractor, he will soon become dissatisfied. But, if he gets to dump the bucket of sawdust after loading it, he is content to rake the sawdust out from under the sawmill and put it in the front-end loader, just so he can drive the tractor a mere 150 feet to dump it. You can't just drive kids; you have to let them steer. Even Laura Rose thinks she is driving the tractor while sitting on my lap with her hands on the wheel.

There are many other things kids can do besides driving a tractor. Give a boy the tools and knowledge to disassemble electronics (and, hopefully, someday reassemble them), and he will love the ship he is on. Give a teenager a job that pays money, and then let him spend it as he pleases, and he will not be leaning over the bow envying others. <u>If you keep your kids on the cutting edge of experience, they will feel sorry for those who do not have their captain and are not on their ship.</u> They will never jump ship. It's the greatest!

Kids need to be able to stand up on that bow and imagine the world to come. This thirteen-year-old boy is building a list of hopes, a vision for the future. He wants to be somebody, do things, go places, live life with a bang. He is developing role models, and I seek to be prominent among them. He has a fine father whom he admires, who does things with him. He is on a different ship, but our ships are running a parallel course; his father and I are sailing to the same destination. For a little while our paths cross, and I, among others, reinforce the values his father is teaching him. He is developing confidence that there is hope in his future; that his dreams can find fulfillment on the ship his father is piloting. This young man will not jump ship if he is confident that the ship he is on is going to deliver him to the shore of his dreams.

If you have a seventeen-year-old whom you treat as a passenger, not allowing him to take significant responsibility and not listening to or instituting his ideas, he will not be content on your ship. He already thinks he is smarter than you are. The only way to prove that he is not is to go along with some of his ideas until they fail; and when they do fail, act surprised and encourage him to try again. Never say, "I told you so." If he is to grow, he must experiment, resulting in both failure and success. Until a man has failed, there is no steel in his bones. Just be thankful that you can be there to facilitate and supervise his endeavors.

GIVING RESPECT

As my boys got into their later teens, I found that upon occasion, they **did** have fresh ideas that were better than my "old
fashioned" way of doing things. The first time a father backs
down from his own position and admits that his son is right is a
time of incomparable bonding and trust. The boy will become
happier and more content than you have seen him since he got
his first shotgun, and you will find him more willing to respect
your wisdom when it is manifest.

My boys and I often discussed issues and concepts: poli-
tics, philosophy, science, war, the Bible, human nature, rocks,
plants, construction. Anything you can think of, we talked
about it. I respected their opinions, even when I disagreed with
them. As they got into their middle and later teens, I could see
in them a growing desire to beat me at anything. I remember
repeatedly challenging my own daddy to arm wrestling until I
could finally beat him. I didn't really want to put him down; I
just wanted his respect, for him to appreciate that I was a man,
just like him. I never "let" my boys beat me at anything. When
Gabriel was about nineteen or twenty years old and six foot
five, I beat him at wrestling. Made him eat sand. It was a great
feeling—a measure of my own seasoned manhood. I am afraid
that now I could no longer take him wrestling. I acknowledge
his strength. Both of the boys now run circles around me in
math. When we are figuring house plans, there is no question
but that I yield to their figures. It doesn't keep me from trying
to catch them in an error. That always helps make my day.

I am making a point about the nature of children, especially
boys. My boys are just like I was when I was young. Your boys
are just like mine. This drive to be respected as a force to be
reckoned with is born in boys, but they need wise direction
when they go through puberty. If your ship provides an outlet

for your sons to express themselves as apprentice captains, and if they see hope that they will not always be just laboring like swabbies on the lower decks, they will stay on your ship with sure expectation of greater things to come.

I see many fathers and mothers resisting their sons' drive to be in control. They are resisting a tsunami. A boy's drive to conquer, lead, and control is in his genes—inevitable. If you are successful in crushing it in a fourteen- or fifteen-year-old, and if you can keep him docile and sweet, you have destroyed his burgeoning manhood. It is a truly sad thing to observe.

PASSENGERS OR CREW MEMBERS?

To be very concise, the sum of our present point is simply: *Children who are treated as passengers instead oft crew members will not be content aboard their ship.* Laura Rose is never a child who is "in the way." The thirteen-year-old boy I've talked about is not just a spectator, told to do his schoolwork, to be quiet, and to stay out of the way until he grows up. He is a man. He is a crew member. When he is with me, I am not just using him; I am training him to be the pilot of a ship, just as Deb is training Laura Rose to be a wife and mother.

Youngsters who see a path to the fulfillment of their dreams will stay the course through the difficult times. They will trust those who have trusted them with positions of responsibility, those who were patient, who taught, encouraged, listened to their dreams and assured them of success. Believing in your children is not a sentiment, nor is it just so many nice words; it is trusting them with responsibility. When a kid feels good about himself because he has triumphed, and you are the one who made it possible, who stood by him, encouraged him, put the rod and reel into his little unbelieving hands, showed him how to make something, how to use the tools, put the key in his hand, taught him how to fly and then stood on the ground and beamed with joy while he soloed, he will always want to be on the ship you are on. He will want to be on the ship that your friends are on. He will want to be part of the armada that is sailing to a new city which has foundations, whose builder and maker is God.

MALE DOMINION

Boys/Men were created by God to exercise dominion and to subdue.

"And God said, Let us make man in our image, after our likeness: and let them have <u>dominion</u> over the fish of the sea, and over the fowl of the air, and over the cattle, and over all the earth, and over every creeping thing that creepeth upon the earth. So God created man in his own image, in the image of God created he him; male and female created he them. And God blessed them, and God said unto them, Be fruitful, and multiply, and replenish the earth, and <u>subdue</u> it: and have <u>dominion</u> over the fish of the sea, and over the fowl of the air, and over every living thing that moveth upon the earth" (Genesis 1:26-28). See also Psalm 8:1-6 and Hebrews 2:7-8.

According to the passages above, it is the very nature of the male to rule in power and glory. It is God's nature to subdue and exercise dominion, and he put that same nature into man. To all of you harried mothers who are fighting your son's emerging manhood, know this, that a man or a boy who does not seek to conquer, rule, and subdue is outside the will of God. His human nature, as given by God, would be in decline. Many mothers have never figured this one out. Problems often occur when a family has birthed and raised three sweet girls before they ever have a son. Mother naturally expects him to be like the girls in personality and temperament. If she tries to force him into the subdued, sensitive role, she will meet with failure, either because he rebels and tries to conquer her, which is his nature, or because she is actually successful in turning him into a sissy, which is the bigger failure.

FATHERS MUST LET GO

Many fathers today are themselves insecure. They never ascended to the place where they felt like they had conquered anything. A man's most rewarding conquest is his woman. If she idolizes him, he will be able to go on and conquer and subdue kingdoms, but if she rebels, he will never be satisfied and may become bitter and reckless and selfish in his pursuit of dominion. Such a father will resist his son's awakening drives to exercise dominion. He feels threatened by his son. When his son challenges him, he takes it personally. The unfulfilled father is desperate to conquer and subdue. For a little while, when his son was four to eight years old, father was the big dog, the conqueror; suddenly, the only little kingdom the father ever ruled was now seeking independence, and he fights it with all his emotion. That father will create a bitter, rebellious teenager. Most movies about teenagers assume this attitude to be the norm.

It is a confident father who can be proud of his sons' growing independence. I raised my children considering the possibility that I could die in the prime of my youth and no longer be an influence in their lives before they were grown. They were raised with the knowledge that they might be removed from my home by the state government at any time, so I taught them self-reliance and independence from the very start. I made sure they knew Bible doctrine, understood the fallacies of evolution and the so-called social sciences to the best of their developing abilities.

The greatest triumph of a teacher is when he is bested by his students. I was at a knife-throwing tournament recently where the expert high scorer bragged that he was recently beaten by one of his students. To some fathers, it is painful to see their sons become capable of pulling away and sailing their own ships. But to the expert knife thrower, it was an added brag that he not only was the champion thrower, he was also the champion teacher.

I say again, your children must have hope that they are on the best ship to prepare them to be captains themselves. They must be challenged at all times, made to feel worthy by the triumphs they experience.

SUBDUE

You must provide the tools and opportunity for your boys to subdue. I remember one day after hard work, my boys decided they wanted to dig a cave in the rocky ridge beside the house. Two of their friends joined them. Four boys between the ages of ten and fourteen dug out five yards of rocky soil in about two hours. It was a mammoth task. If I had made them do it for some valid reason, it would have taken them three or more grudging days, but when they were working toward their own vision, it was all play. Do you understand boys? Do you really understand men? That piece of hard ground had been lying there in defiance ever since Noah's flood. It needed to be taught a lesson. It needed to be conquered, subdued, made to serve them. They beat it. They won. The "trophy" hole is still there today. They never returned to it after "conquering" it that day, because it no longer served a purpose; but did they ever benefit from the digging of it!

A boy takes a BB gun out and stalks helpless little pretty birds all day long. Finally, he kills one. He plucks out the prettiest and longest feathers and sticks them in his hat. "…dominion over the birds of the air…"

I remember as a boy how I loved to go down to the ditch that ran under the road close to the house, and there I would fish for crawfish. We called them "crawdads." There was a pool of water there about eight feet across and eighteen inches deep. It was full of the defiant little creatures with their hard shells and snappy pinchers. Over several years I perfected my technique for catching them. I would put them in a bucket and show them off to my highly appreciative and admiring friends. It was a big brag to catch a colossal, red crawfish that everyone was afraid to pick up. When they had all tried and lost their nerve, I would carefully pick up the monster and hold it up at eye level for all to see. To get further admiration, I would tease the creature with the other hand, tempting him to snap shut on my finger. "…dominion over the fish of the sea…"

When I was a young teenager, I would catch poisonous snakes and skin them out to make hatbands. Talk about gaining respect from the guys! "…dominion over every thing that creepeth upon the earth…"

The building of the pyramids in Egypt by the pharaohs was clearly an exercise of dominion, their "bragging" monuments. Even girls have a "quarter measure" of this dominion pursuit in them. They are nest builders. They don't care to rope a bear, but they will take a little corner of the world and turn it into a home for their men and their children. My girls loved to build dwelling places. They would stack logs in the woods to make a house. They would decorate a treehouse that the boys built, or they would take a corner of the barn and turn it into a dining room where they would serve tea.

The physical world offers endless challenges to the male population. It is primarily men who chase tornadoes, seeing

31

how close they can get, and photographing themselves doing so as proof of their prowess. Men are attracted to violent,
belching volcanoes, high mountains, and the dangerous depths
of the sea.

One of the Russian boys who stays with us during the summer months just got a new bicycle today. A few moments ago
he came in with a badly banged up knee. He had jumped his
bicycle off the porch. Anybody can ride on flat ground, but to
sail through the air, to land without crashing (hopefully), and
to get up and try something higher next time—wow!!! What a
thrill to defy the law of gravity, conquer, and subdue! I didn't
tell him not to try it again. He's learning something difficult
and challenging. Let him put his face to the wind and discover
his own powers and his limitations. All famous inventors were
people who didn't believe in established limitations. Their
God-given drive to exercise dominion and to subdue was not
limited by what others believed.

If you are going to keep your children happy and satisfied
being on your ship, you must provide for the full expression
of their dominion drives. There is much more to it than this,
but kids have jumped ship for less. Take your son to the pilot-
house when he is only three months old and put his hands on
the wheel; imagine him piloting the ship while you sleep, and
then train him to do so.

CHAPTER 3

MAINTAINING MORALE

Dear Mr. Pearl,

I was one of those children who jumped ship, and I did so for all the reasons you listed. My parents were hypocrites and expected the same from my sister and me. Our family was the perfect Pharisee household, although we "prodigal daughters" tainted that appearance. We never missed a church service; we always helped in church ministry, always witnessed to our neighbors, and kept the Sabbath day holy (if you didn't count the fighting or abuse that went on behind our closed doors). Believe me, we had everyone fooled. When my sister jumped ship, I went back and told one of my mother's friends the truth of what our family was really like. She didn't believe me—I'm telling you we hid the hypocrisy very well. We did not tell, mostly out of fear of more anger and abuse that would come if we let it be known. Pride kept us strong, not God.

I jumped ship for two reasons. The first was to escape home, and I figured I might as well give them something to condemn me for since they were going to condemn me regardless of what I did. Also, part of me longed to know the good Shepherd and to lie down in green pastures. I had to jump ship because I was DETER-MINED NEVER to become a Pharisee like my parents—I had to flee. My sister had no choice but to do as I did. Our parents still say it was our choice and they had nothing to do with it!

They are so blinded by religion and are confident that they trained us right, but that, due to some fault in us, did not work. Just this past week they were proclaiming that we will one day come around to their way of thinking.

I love living in the grace I have found in Christ! I love that my kids love me, that my husband and I love each other; I love that I am free to choose joy and hope every day.

I can attest to the fact that when children are not engaged as vital crew members on a glorious voyage, they do acquire a greater sin than "rebellion." They become angry, bitter, resentful human beings who are beaten down, broken, and will lash out at all attempts to be loved. Like a runaway dog that was abused all the time, when you try to feed him, he will bite you because he was trained to expect evil.

Beka was right—it is all about love. You were right—it is all about joy. And where does that come from? It comes from knowing Jesus. I wish my parents could really know Him. God

*has used you to reach so many, for which I am
grateful, and I look forward one day to know
that my kids know Him also.*

AB

GOOD CHILDREN GROW OUT OF GOOD SOIL.

There it is! The primary reason children jump ship is because parents make the voyage miserable. Facing that fact is
the first step to recovery. When they are trained right, they walk
right. And you should know by now that training is much more
than words and warnings, more than principles and precepts.
When the example is wrong, the words can never be right
enough, because our attitude screams louder than our words.

Parenting is the most accurate test of one's true character.
It reveals the fountainhead of all that lies within the parents'
heart and soul and uncovers all that is hidden. Children reflect
the soul of their parents; they manifest the heart that has been
formally concealed behind sophisticated screens and carefully crafted public perceptions. We parents can manipulate the
public perceptions, leading others to believe we are something
quite different from reality. But it is our children who become
windows to our true selves, often opening the windows wider
than we would like and at times we do not expect. They find
and expose the real you and tap into and follow that reality as
their guide. They bypass our words and emulate our vital cen-
ters. If their mother has a "bad" day, all the children will have a
bad day, and Dad will have a bad evening. Bad days make bad
weeks and bad months and bad years, which eventually turn
into bad lives.

It is impossible to become a good parent without experiencing a revival within. There can be no duplicity. Parenting
is not like a job where you meticulously follow the procedures

of your job description and then clock out, knowing that you have played your part well enough, even though your heart wasn't in it. You can't do the right thing as a parent without being the right person. Your children are just too perceptive to be fooled by outward displays. When parents have a trans-formation within, good parenting comes naturally, without all the struggle and deliberation. Pure souls living pure lives don't need a great deal of knowledge about child training to raise good kids. Good children grow out of good parental soil.

America needs revival. The Christian church needs revival. The homeschool family needs revival. Most of all, parents need revival, because the children won't survive the Sodom in which we live without a revival that changes us from the inside out.

SO, WHAT CAN I DO?

Many people have written, some of them just a little bit irritated, saying, "OK, there is a problem; my own children are near to jumping ship, so tell us what to do. Give us some practical examples." They are missing the point. It is not about *doing*; it is about *being*. Get real! Love God with all your heart and soul and mind and strength until the joy of the Lord fills your cup to overflowing. Fall back in love with your spouse (that's the first fruit of revival!), and enjoy each other in front of the kids! Let the Holy Spirit create discipline in you so that you use your time wisely and have more time to be with your children. It is a matter of perspective—of where your heart is actually fixed.

Parenting is the most demanding job in the universe. The CEO of a mega company needs to excel in a limited number of areas only, but to be an effective parent requires expertise in many areas. And, more than any other job—more than being a pastor or missionary—it requires purity of soul.

Nearly everyone comes to parenting with a lot of counterproductive concepts. If God gave us a parenting test before allowing us to have babies, few homes would have a swing set or a box of toys. Unfortunately, it almost seems that it is first necessary to become a parent in order to learn to be a parent, and most of you may learn too late to do your children any good. Most obstacles that limit children's potential are set in motion by the parents and are rooted in their own fears, ego needs, and inattentiveness. But parents are most often blinded by their ego and careless, unproductive habits.

Thankfully, we don't have to be perfect people, or even especially wise, to become good parents. Nor do we need to be thoroughly informed as to all the ins and outs of parenting as taught in books or by enrolling in parenting classes. We don't need schooling. We need to be real—consistently real—and caring. We need to be there, right in the midst of our children—in their face, if you will. Everything else will somehow fall into place when our hearts are right. A right heart can make up for a lot of wrong-headedness, but great knowledge and understanding can never make up for indifference. Genuine love will cover a multitude of sins.

GREAT HOPE

There is great hope here. Think of it this way: To be a successful parent, you don't have to suddenly be all wise—to know what to do in the many varied situations; rather, by simply having a good heart and a proper attitude, your children will respond positively to you. Love and respect will fill in all the voids left by inexperience and ignorance.

You will get a much better response from your children when they perceive that you care more about them than you do about public perception. They are more perceptive than you give them credit for, and they always know your true heart—even when you don't want them to. Your children must be conscious that you really want them to have great experiences. When they see you putting emotional energy into them, they will respond with cooperation and openness. They will be moved by your willingness to invest yourself in their lives. Think of yourself as raising up a manager for your own company—someone to take your place when you are absent, and to assume your position when you are gone and no longer part of the equation. Your children are your legacy, the only one that will endure in future generations. Working together toward common goals eliminates that adversarial relationship that poisons most families and sabotages every good effort.

Sudden changes of heart with big efforts will not impress them. A lot of small gestures add up to big trust. You will create a climate of trust by never hurting them at "heart level"—but always demonstrating a caring spirit.

RESPECT AND DIGNITY

You say that you want to know what to DO? Respect your children. *Your respect of them grants you the dignity you feel you should have.* Respect is not just a perspective; it is a chain of events resulting from a chain of individual acts. Demonstrate your respect by allowing your teenagers to make a positive impact on the home and their younger siblings. And you can especially demonstrate respect by listening to their ideas and treating them with the same seriousness you treat this book you are now reading. Talk to them, and then listen. Share your worldviews in a relaxed, non-instructive manner. Talk about your likes and define your weaknesses. Ask for help. Ask their opinion on something like how to resolve an interpersonal relationship in the church or at work. When you talk to them personally, and they can sense that their answers and opinions count, they will follow suit. Talk and listen. You often have to listen to the irrelevant for a while before children will get down to the issues that are important. They will not just walk up and say, "I need your advice." They test the waters to see if they are welcomed before they jump in with the big stuff. Listen. Always listen. The last thing many parents hear as their kids are going over the railing is, "You didn't listen to me." If you make excuses by telling me how hard you tried to parent them and how much you care, then I will have to join your teenager and say, "You didn't listen to me either". It doesn't matter what you think about how you performed. It doesn't matter how you interpret your intentions. The reality you must work with is the one your teenager sees. What do they think? What have they said to you? That's reality.

One of the problems with us parents is that we fail to adjust to the fast-growing changes in our children. They want recognition and respect before we realize it is important to them. One day they are simply childish, and the next day they are childish acting with an adult's need for equal respect. When we shut them out of the adult world until they demonstrate that they are ready for it, they feel mistreated and misunderstood. In sports, it is like having to put them on the team's first string, starting the game in key positions, when you know they're not ready for it yet. But they want to play ball so bad, even if they are going to strike out or miss a fly ball. If you keep them on the bench until they are ready, they will join another team or go play another game—like a game of craps with some low life "team members" who don't demand so much from them.

NEVER BELITTLING

Never, never, never belittle their efforts or debase their person. Some parents' leadership style is to demean, to cast their children in a role of unworthiness with the mistaken belief that it is the children's responsibility to prove *by their works* that they are indeed worthy. Thankfully, God doesn't deal with us that way. And you as their parents shouldn't either! Your role must change from warden to friend. Remember Jesus' words to His disciples: "Henceforth I call you not servants; for the servant knoweth not what his lord doeth: but I have called you friends; for all things that I have heard of my Father I have made known unto you" (John 15:15). None of us perform well for those who do not believe in us. But we will kill ourselves trying to live up to the best expectations of those who believe we can do anything and whom we know will be tolerant of our mistakes and shortcomings.

Let me say it another way. If a child does a bad thing, or many bad things, don't fall for the lie that he is a bad child. If you talk to him as though he is bad, in hopes that he will try to be good, you will achieve the opposite. Find a good thing in your child and speak of it. If you instill in him that he is your "good" boy, those good vibes will enable him to want to cultivate that feeling and he will resist being a bad boy.

COMMAND AND (TOO MUCH) CONTROL

Some parents settle for too little, controlling only the outward behavior of their children, but not equipping their souls. They are forceful in their discipline and do indeed train their younger children to obey at home and perform well in public, but fail to equip them with independent decision-making skills

40

and character. You can keep children in baby seats and later belt them into wheelchairs so they will not fall down and break a limb, a sure guarantee of their safety, but it will not teach them to run with the ball and get back up after suffering the hard knocks that life will throw their way.

Children will not be content to be protected and guarded. If you squeeze too hard, they will slip out of your grasp as sure as a wet bar of soap.

It is emotionally taxing on us parents to expose our children to the dangers of working as a crew member on life's ship. We want to protect and guard them against sudden waves and slippery decks, but they must be allowed to get their sea legs and learn the ropes of life, or they will not only be unprepared for life, they will be extremely unhappy as passengers.

Include your children in serious decisions, starting at around age two. Find ways to cause them to reason through problems with you. Discuss the issues, and then describe the ramifications of different scenarios. This is homeschooling—soul schooling. It is graduate-level preparation for life. Mama says to six-year-old Linda, "This article I am reading says that eating sugar causes yeast build up in the body." Explain in simple terms the symptoms and consequences of yeast infections. "Do you think we ought to stop eating this cereal with the sugar in it?" You have already made up your mind, but you are going to include her in the decision-making loop. When she decides that it is not wise, you will not have trouble taking her favorite cereal away from her. When the horrible stories you tell her and the example of the sick lady at church convince her to lay off the sugar, you have led her to practice self- denial, and to make consequential and painful decisions. You are building character. This is respect. This is treating your child with dignity.

If you have never included your twelve-year-old in character decisions and you suddenly thrust options upon her, don't
be surprised if she brushes the responsibility aside and chooses
the sugar. It will take time. Work your way up to serious shar-
ing of responsibility in increments that the child can handle.

WORK

What can you do to keep your children happy on your ship?
Teach them to work. The most miserable people are those with
no responsibility. People are happiest when someone depends
on them.

The secret to teaching children to work is to start them off
on jobs that they will enjoy carrying out. If there is no such
job for a particular child, then structure a job with other incen-
tives—like fellowship (working *with* someone), or work of a
shorter duration—that will make the work pleasant. On a ship,
one of the first concerns of the captain is the morale of the crew.
When optimism and hope run high, the ship is prepared for any
eventuality. Think about the difference it would make if you had
eight initiative-takers instead of eight foot-draggers. Give attention to their morale. Never keep pushing if the family has lost its
morale. Intimidation may cause fear and bring outward compli-
ance, but it will never cause productivity or contentment.

Avoid slave labor. I tried to gauge the physical and emotional stamina of each child and to never push them beyond their
level of tolerance. The thin line is to increase their threshold for
the pain of work without making them feel like slaves. The
pain of work is softened by working with someone in fellowship. Drudgery is diminished by doing a job that is challenging
and creative. Work can be better endured when it produces a
suitable reward, and it can be tolerated if it has a foreseeable
end. Productive children are happy children.

PURPOSE

The family's morale will skyrocket when they clearly understand the purpose for their existence. Only then will they cooperate and accept the sacrifices of labor without bickering. I remember one time, not long after getting married, my father-in- law invited me to help him do some plumbing. The plumbing turned out to be uncovering a septic tank buried in hard ground. After I had picked and shoveled in the summer heat for about two hours and dug a hole about two feet deep, widening it several times, looking for the tank, he calmly suggested that I try digging ten feet further west. After digging another hour, he suggested that we move over and try another test hole. Now, the first hole was a miserable dig, but I bore it without complaint because I thought it had a purpose that would soon be realized. However, when it became clear that he was using me in the place of a backhoe to prospect for a tank, the location of which he hadn't the foggiest idea, I lost all commitment to his "vision." Digging is always bad enough; digging without purpose or progress is unacceptable. I suddenly remembered an appointment I had elsewhere. I dropped my pick, and told him to hire a backhoe. Aha! you might say, "I jumped ship." If it were my septic tank, I would have hired equipment to do that awful work. He wasn't digging. He was watching me and making suggestions. It was demeaning to have my time and energies valued in that manner. If, at that point, my father-in-law had possessed the power to make me keep working, and had done so, I would have "hated" him for it. He is eighty years old as I write this, and I think I will go and tell him one more time what a dumb idea that was. We laugh about it now, but it wasn't funny thirty-five years ago in the heat of August.

I hope you haven't gotten lost in my personal story and missed the point. Kids will wear themselves out for you when they can see and enjoy the success of their labors, but when you try to force slavery upon them, they will file the chains off their ankles and jump ship.

BOREDOM

Boredom is the mother of invention, but if not addressed as an opportunity, it can also be the "devil's workshop" or the cauldron of emotional disturbance. When boredom drags on like an incessant winter rain, kids and parents will work up a good fight just to create a little excitement and flood the brain with a few endorphins. "It beats smelling your breath and looking at your ugly face."

"Don't touch me. Tell him not to touch me."

"Get out of my room."

"I had that chair first."

"I think I will just lie down for a while. You kids, go watch a video."

The captain of any ship knows to keep his deck hands busy at all times, allowing them just enough time to eat and sleep. They will clean and paint and repair and then do it again, for boredom eats morale like fungus eats wet wood.

Boredom is eliminated by commitment to a mission. To put it simply, when you have something to do that must be done, or that you want to do, you will never be attacked with the giant sloth of boredom.

People who are bored do not like themselves, and they do not like others. They don't like life. Bored kids are pouty, unhappy, self-condemning, ungrateful, and unlikable.

You can organize away boredom, in your own life as well as the kids. Design a creative agenda, hour by hour if need be. Obtain the tools of creativity—musical instruments, paints, color crayons and colored chalk, sewing, cooking, gardening, construction, mechanics, animals (cows, horses, sheep, chickens, pigs), herbs, reading, and a thousand other things. Take every opportunity to learn and grow with your children. Don't impose your ideas of creativity on them. Just experiment until something takes with one of the kids, and then keep experimenting until all the children have been captured with some consuming interest. It is better to be interested in something frivolous than in nothing at all. If you have a girl who likes to collect baby doll clothes, become enthusiastic about it and stop by the yard sales and junk stores to help feed her interest and supply her collection. Kids will stay on a ship just to finish a project. If you love what they love, they will love you for it. One of the best things you can do for your kids is to feed their creativity.

ENTHUSIASM

The family should be constantly full of enthusiastic energy. Energy is more attitude than metabolism. Enthusiasm of ideas is a fountain of energy. If your mind is excited by ideas, your body will respond with strength to match. Most sickliness grows out of the ooze of indifference to life. If you just let life happen to you, you will be like a can kicked down the sidewalk by a bored kid. Stop whining and assigning blame. Get up and construct life to your liking. If you as a parent feel like a kicked can in life, your kids will be kicked cans. Become a builder, a maker, a doer. God is a creator, and we, in his image, are creators as well. Your kids must be growing, or they will be going somewhere more interesting and challenging where they can grow.

Enthusiasm is a zest for life. It is unrelenting belief that you **are** going to be productive in some way. It is accepting the challenge and setting forth to conquer. Your kids need to see your enthusiasm for life. It will rub off on them. Enthusiasm just feels good, and they will want to be a part of it. Get a project—no, ten projects—and try to do all of them at once. Some will never get done. Some will never even get started. But occasionally, one of your harebrained ideas will become a monument to the cooperation and productivity of your family, and the kids will never forget it.

Dig up the crooked cobblestones in the old walkway, and re-lay them into a pleasing pattern with some new additions that are creative. It will take you and the kids about two weeks. Make sure that they are not your "slave labor". Work together, and let them do some of the creative work, even if it is not done as well as it otherwise could have been.

Re-stucco and repaint the swimming pool. Put up a new mailbox, and let the kids paint and decorate it. Make curtains. Refinish the floor. You've got the idea. Enthusiasm and fun are synonymous.

RESPONSIBILITY

Children will not be happy if they are not given increasing responsibility. When you give children responsibility, you may be signing on for a dispensation of mediocrity. What two-year-old sweeps the floor and washes dishes perfectly? What ten-year-old boy paints the screen door like a pro? Children in a home are like loose bowling balls riding in the back of a pickup truck; you never start or stop any project or turn a corner without a few bumps, and maybe a little damage to the house.

It is difficult for us 'accomplished' adults, especially those who are controlled by the demon of perfectionism, to allow their children to participate in the finished product. We can do it so much better. Why would I label the desire to do everything perfectly, a demon? Because those who are given to this habit are known to place order first and other people second. Perfectionists are often depressed or angry when someone does not respect their need to "have a place for everything and to put everything in its place." Perfectionists are selfish persons who should get themselves bronzed and stuck in a museum on a shelf with other figurines. They are no good in a house full of kids.

Any construction project generates a lot of noise, dust, clutter, and garbage. It is the cost of progress. The home is a construction site, a place where children are being molded into adults, and where adults are fitted for service.

The difference between a child and an adult is the ability to take full responsibility. A physically grown man who is not emotionally equipped to assume responsibility is a pathetic child in an adult body. It is our calling as parents to transition our children from irresponsible, selfish consumers to mature, responsible adults. It doesn't happen automatically, and there is a need in the soul of every child to become increasingly responsible. Those who are not made accountable in this regard tend toward self-loathing and despondency on the one hand, and bullying and licentiousness on the other, depending on their degree of boldness and disregard for authority. Either way, their lives will be embedded in discontentment, making them a ship-jumping waiting to happen.

I have met several homeschool boys—young men eighteen to thirty years old—who were useless as adults. It is as though their bodies have been growing for years, but their brains were just recently implanted. They are innocent, pure in body and mind, but no one would think of them as being of good character, for they are as untested as a six-week-old puppy in a

Frisbee-catching contest. They stand around waiting for someone to tell them what to do. They are the first ones that you
don't trust on the Internet. They grew up without being given
responsibility.

First make your children responsible to oversee their younger siblings. I know that there is a ship-jumping in the future
when parents express shock that I would suggest that their ten-
year-old should be encouraged to discipline his six- year old
brother. When I see a sixteen-year-old who resists associating
with her younger siblings, I know that her parents have not given
her responsibility over them. She sees their wayward acts when
Mother is occupied elsewhere, and she is frustrated with their
non-compliance. The younger children have learned that she is
a paper tiger; she has eyes to see and mouth to complain, but she
has no teeth. Mother even "protects" the younger children from
her, treating her as if she were the problem. They have learned
to abuse or misuse her in subtle ways, knowing that she will be
sternly rebuked if she fights back. The sixteen-year-old can't
wait to get out of the home and away from these "little brats".

When parents hear me say these things, they object, "But
my sixteen-year-old is not mature enough to "mother" her
brothers and sisters; she is a problem child herself and part of
the problem." As President Reagan once said, "There you go
again." Many parents have heard my advice and gone home
to inform their younger children that older sister is now the
second Mama, and that they will have to obey her. She is even
allowed to administer light spankings to the very young children—say, those under five. She is allowed to deny the others
certain privileges.

It is understood by all the children that the parents are still
the last court of appeal. The sixteen-year-old is bound to make

some wrong decisions along the way, but haven't we all? That is part of learning.

Many parents have come back to tell me that after placing their morose, rebellious teenager in charge of her younger siblings, she took her position of responsibility very seriously and rose to the occasion by trying to be fair and just and merciful in all her dealings with them. She showed maturity overnight. And within days, she was liking them, and they were respecting her. An amazing side effect happened, as well: Affection developed between them. Responsibility demands and produces the best in all of us. It is like a magnet pulling us toward maturity.

Take time to sit down with your older kids, and ask their opinion on training the younger kids. Listen to their comments. Respect their opinions. Be sure to let them know that you are not only going to use their good ideas, but that you want them to incorporate them into their own dealings with the younger children. And, thank them for being a help to you. They will be among those who know how to swim **before** they hit the water.

We humans are by nature always in need of reaching higher, stretching just beyond our abilities. And we are not happy unless we're regularly doing so. Give your teens all the responsibility they can handle, and then step back and let them try. Define the parameters in which they are allowed to operate, and then set them free to experiment, including failing (without fear of punishment).

Trust is a powerful incentive. Create an atmosphere that allows a child who makes a mistake to admit to it and take responsibility without recrimination. He can then use his energies to improve his performance, rather than falling into the self-defeating trap of excuse-making. Kids make excuses when the consequences don't allow any way out. Provide a setting in which they can start fresh, and with experiences that will enable them not to make the same mistake again.

RESPECTING AUTHORITY

Authority is a fact of life. It is truly an innate characteristic of humanity. We were created to be under authority, free within the limits of the rule of law, but bound to observe that authority above us which represents justice and order. All legitimate authority comes from God, according to Romans chapter thirteen, even secular authority. Children learn to respect your authority when they see you respecting the authorities above you. Your disrespect of authority above breeds disrespect for your authority from below. Disdain for authority in general springs from rank egotism.

There are times in history when the place of authority was usurped by evil men for evil purposes. At such times that "authority" was to be resisted, not out of a spirit of pride, but rather out of allegiance to justice and respect for human dignity. Children must see your respect, even reverence, for authority, and if the need should ever arise to challenge authority, they should see your caution and reluctance to do so. Only then can you hope to be respected by them in the same degree. It is imperative that mothers do not undermine fathers' authority, and that younger children do not see their older siblings disregarding parents' authority. Likewise, if your children see you acting contrary to the authority you are under—church, employer, local law enforcement, etc., they will feel free to not support you when they disagree with your policies.

The reason for this general dissertation on authority should be obvious to the point of this book; there are times on your family ship when the storms obscure the goals and all seems hopeless. When that happens, it is respect for authority that keeps everybody on course until things calm down and morale can be restored. Kids have been known to suddenly jump ship and quickly suffer irreparable damage, only to admit a week later that they made a hasty and stupid mistake.

In addition, parents must live and conduct themselves in a manner that elicits respect for, and trust in, their authority. It is beyond all reason to demand that a growing child respect an authority that is not respectable. It is hard enough to keep them honoring the honorable, but to expect them to honor the repugnant and evil is a reach too far.

ELEVATING YOUR CHILDREN

There is a human tendency that is wrong-headed—achieving the opposite of what is intended. You may have an employee who is not performing well, so rather than just tell him, you start picking at him, insinuating things, making cutting remarks to him here and there. You are not as friendly to him as you are to the others. You are more aloof, not joking or laughing with him. He is treated as though he is guilty of something. You are hoping he will take the hint and do better. No, he will quit just to get out from under the condemnation. You probably justify your actions in that part of your mind where you respect your own sense of fair play by telling yourself that this pressure you are applying is designed to get him to work harder to be acceptable—to do what he ought, of course. But he will not perform better just to please you, or even to keep his job, for the heart is taken out of him by the atmosphere you have created. He hates the company, hates everything it stands for, and he will leave in a dark mist of rejection, never to be your friend under any circumstances. Forty years later, when your name is mentioned, or when he sees you old and bent over in a Wal-Mart, he will hope you had a miserable life. Yes, his performance was unacceptable, but you did not treat him as a person. You actually divested him of the emotional energy that he would need to improve his performance. You broke his morale.

I can feel your pain, for I can feel my own, having treated people that way in the past. Are we stupid, or what? But the people we have hurt and rejected have gone their way. We are not likely to see them again, and we can forget, and hope that they can, too. We also hope that we didn't matter enough to them to permanently scar them in any way.

My painful remarks have just been preparation for personal surgery. Get ready for the knife. Have you related to your child in a similar way? Have you shut her out, withheld yourself, criticized, letting her see your disapproval, hoping she would take the necessary steps to win your favor and earn your approval? I will say it again, having spoken and written it many times, "No one ever climbed out from under a pile of disapproval to win the favor of his or her accuser." Your child will do just what the employee did; she will flee from your presence at the earliest opportunity. She will jump ship, even if there are sharks in the water. Better to be chewed up by sharks than to be chewed out every day.

You know when you are in the presence of someone dedicated to elevating you. And, you also know when someone with a hidden agenda proceeds to tear you down, to humble you, to see you admit that you are wrong, and to make you try harder to win their approval. You naturally don't want to be around them. No doubt they think they are on a mission of righteousness, that they have a calling from God to hold up a higher standard, and you are their mission field. It stinks, doesn't it?

Your children may have the same reaction to the way you treat them. Think about it.

Instead of tearing your children down to make them submissive to your commands, build them up so you don't have to give them commands. Your job as a parent and the principal educator is to create a climate that enables them to unleash their potential. Given the right environment, you will be surprised at what they are capable of achieving.

Our constant drive should be to make them grow taller, to elevate them, not with flattering words, but with space to grow, and the opportunity to fail and try again, all without shame or embarrassment. When your children see you taking pleasure in helping them develop and grow, they will take pleasure in doing the same with their siblings and with others. When they feel you have been patient with their failures, they will be patient with yours. When your children are hard on you, know for a certainty that you have been hard on them.

STARTING OVER

Raise your kids as if your getting to heaven were based on their good works and good attitudes. How are you measuring up? Do you want to get down to the bitter root? Ask them, "What do you like most...least about our home?; what would you change if you could?" The answer will give you a chance to reexamine your own policies and attitudes, as well as to provide an opportunity to instruct your children in ways that will give them fresh perspectives on your goals and your reasons. When you listen to your children, you will come to respect them more as people, and they will more willingly go along with your policies without grumbling, knowing that they have been heard and their views considered. They will greatly appreciate it when you find out what their goals are and then help them to get there. There is creativity and growth infused into the family by providing information and clarifying it. Those children who have it prosper. Those who don't stagnate. They have hopes and dreams and desire to understand why what they are doing is important, i.e., how it relates to the big picture. Optimism and pessimism are both contagious. When one member of the family gets one or the other, it tends to spread to all. God's intention is for parents to be the ones to exhibit optimism, because their children will see it as the hope they so desire for themselves in their future. Infecting your children with a spirit of optimism will pay many dividends in your and their future.

REPENT, OR WATCH YOUR CHILDREN PERISH

This writer understands that there is more preacher and prophet in him than therapist. I do not seek to make you feel good about yourself. My goal is not to encourage you, but to inform you of your failures and to call you to repentance before God. It would be gratifying if, in reading my remarks, you would learn at least one more helpful principle or technique and successfully apply it to your children's training. But, if you would simply repent and become a disciple of the man from Nazareth, if you were filled with the Holy Spirit of God, you would always have One to teach you, and there would be a sudden and radical shift in your entire life—including your relationship to your children. There it is, nothing held back. I cannot do otherwise.

CHAPTER 4

PROVIDE ENTERTAINMENT

"All work and no play makes Jack a dull boy," so says the popular children's rhyme. "No play" will also make Jack very dissatisfied with the ship he is on, and when he gets old enough, he will observe the gaiety of others and begin to think about jumping ship for one that is more fun. If you are going to prevent your children from longingly looking at other passing vessels, you must meet their need for diversion and entertainment. It is true that if left to themselves, children will overdose on entertainment, and, like Pinocchio, they will come to ruin on Pleasure Island. Yet, even with that danger in mind, the fact remains that children, just like adults, have a legitimate emotional need to indulge in playful fun.

Mature, well-adjusted adults live to produce, and, to everyone except a fisherman, recreational play is clearly secondary, whereas small children live to play ("when I was a child, I thought as a child"). Children would never work if not trained and constrained to do so. During their first twenty years, they evolve from a full-time life of play to full-time working. There is also a rapid transition in their forms of play. In a period of fifteen years, they will go from tasting everything on the floor to riding motor cycles in competitions, or competing in international chess games. It becomes increasingly difficult for parents to keep up with their children's changing interests. I now clearly understand why God chose to give babies to young people and not to us old folks. It takes a lot of energy to meet their ever-changing and increasing needs.

The key to providing proper and adequate entertainment is that you must *thoroughly enjoy* seeing them immersed in good healthy fun. Children have always loved pushing or riding something. They love the thrill of simple things, like sliding down a steep, grassy hill on a piece of cardboard, or sledding on snow and skating on ice. Kids love wheels, even at the earliest age, and will continue to do so until eventually they are begging to take "your wheels" out for a joyride. I just love putting one-year-olds on plastic riding toys and teaching them to push themselves along with their feet. They soon graduate to a tricycle and then on to a bicycle. Can you remember their thrill when they first rode without training wheels, and how exhilarated they were when they mastered roller skates, skateboards, and. . .skies—and the faster the better?

When I was a kid, my daddy assisted me by bringing home old wagon wheels and axles and scrap boards. Lawn mower wheels are excellent. At eight years old, along with the rest of the neighbor kids, I would build what we called a go-cart—something with four wheels, a seat, and a way to steer it, but no motor. Dad would bring home buckets with the remnants of bright-colored paints, and we would paint our push cars to be the snazziest in the neighborhood. Then we would find a hill where the road was momentarily empty of cars, and, while one person rode and steered, the other would push him as fast as legs could go. It was then "freewheeling" it to the bottom of the hill to see whose car was the fastest. Yes, there was many a wreck, and the pusher would sometimes fall flat on his face in the road. And, yes, occasionally the cars would turn over or crash into the ditch or into each other. But, the "challenge and the thrill" is what made it all *so much fun.*

My parents played their parts quite well. Daddy provided the raw material and an occasional suggestion as to improvements in the design. Mama was fitly admiring of my paint job and ingenuity. Grandma liked to watch the races, especially if there was a crash. To finally get Dad to sit on our masterpiece of a push car and let us push him was the ultimate thrill. And to see him sitting there so vulnerable and so stiff and scared just added more to our "great" achievement.

After I was grown and married and had kids of my own, I got my old daddy in the passenger seat of my newly designed third rail buggy sometimes called a "dune buggy"—made from a Volkswagen Beetle. I got him strapped in with the jet airplane safety harness, and then took it up to about forty and put it into a spin, with the obvious risk of turning over. He was scared to death, and I loved it. When I jumped it over a hill and got airborne for about sixty feet, he started screaming and then we really started having fun. At least I did. Before long, he was driving it by himself (I was scared to ride with him after what I had put him through), and he spun out into a swamp, soaking himself and the buggy. We had loads of fun that day.

Times change and toys change, but children remain the same. They have an inherent need to tackle challenges and turn them into thrills. They will climb to the top of the tallest tree, jump into the water from the highest spot they dare, and then later they will want to see how fast the family car will go. It is dangerous being a kid, and it always has been, but to them it is just sheer fun. We adults must provide restraint and caution while we still can, before they get big enough to get out of our sight too quickly. But play they will, and play will inevitably find the thrill in everything, whether it is a ten-month-old climbing to the top of the stairs, or a ten-year-old climbing to the top of the fire tower, or a twenty-year-old checking out hang gliding.

GIRLS PLAY

Girls start off playing much like the boys, but with a little less of the thrill seeking. They love horses and bicycles, but they also enjoy practicing to be mothers. Young girls, right down to the one-year-olds, entertain themselves with playing house and family. "Mama Pearl", my wife, just bought a two-foot-long broom for ten-month-old Gracie. She spends a lot of time "sweeping" the floor. Almost three-year-old Laura Rose has her own little china tea set. She will spend an hour playing with the dishes and pouring tea for everyone. When my daughters were six years old, they would bake something and expect the whole world to stop and indulge in their delectable delight. I was delighted with them for their many attempts, even when I often had to pretend to swallow and then slip outside unnoticed to get rid of the unpleasant mouthful.

Parents who habitually push their children aside, not wanting to be bothered with their frivolous play, will lose the hearts of their children. It is not enough to allow time for your children to play; you must "sacrifice" your time and yourself and play with them. You don't have to physically be there at the swing set all the time, but they must feel that your eyes are watching them from the kitchen window. You can even stop your work and run outside occasionally to laugh at them or to be "amazed" at their abilities.

I sought to be the most thrilling source of entertainment available to my kids. I actually pushed them to do the daring things. I helped them set up a jump for their bicycles, encouraged them to swing higher, do flips off of the rope swing into the pond, or do difficult dives from the diving board. I took them skating, and we raced around the rink. When it snowed, which was only once or twice a year in Memphis, I stopped everything I was doing just to play with them. We would make a sled and go find the highest hill. We would even try at full speed to make it through the sharpest curve, and "piled up" time and time again until we finally got it right. We were rightly proud of ourselves and congratulated each other profusely.

At times, I took the boys into the swamps where we regularly caught or killed snakes, and caught sacks full of fish. We speared the very large fish or shot them with arrows. Exploring new "uncharted" territory was exciting, something we greatly enjoyed. I practiced baseball with the boys until they were good enough to not be embarrassed playing on a local team. But one season was enough for them. They liked the wild places much better, and throwing knives filled in the empty spots between their exciting outings with me.

We had a pond for the kids to swim in, but they would get bored swimming alone by themselves and started begging me to join them. When I headed toward the pond, they all got excited, and the ones who were not already in the pond would rush to join us. They knew I was going to add a new dimension to the fun, even though it might be nothing more than my watching and laughing as they did some new stunt in the water.

SOCIAL LIFE

Now, important as it is to be involved with your children in their younger years, the most critical time for entertainment is when they get to their middle teens. At around fifteen years old, their social life becomes a significant part of their entertainment, and, in many cases, it is their primary concern. Social entertainment has the potential of impacting them very negatively and is much more demanding of discerning parents. It is at this point that many parents make the mistake of trying to completely fence off their growing teens from other young people, lest they do something foolish and destructive, either physically or morally.

When my kids were getting into their early teens, I set up a volleyball net in the "holler" back of the house and invited other families to join us. Girls and boys their own age came to play. We were always there to oversee the kids together. They got to socialize with the opposite sex naturally, and without resorting to the dating pattern so common in modern society.

I will be quite plain about the social life of teenagers. When kids go through puberty, especially boys, mating becomes a consuming interest. They begin to live in a daydream/night-dream world. You can't prevent it. It is absolutely natural, and is quite glorious and wonderful. It is God's design, intended to cause them to want to marry and reproduce. Furthermore, by divine design, the sexual drive constitutes the most controlling temptation a boy or man will ever face. It is the ultimate test of character and the bedrock on which self-control can be established. On this single pivotal point, young men either shipwreck, sometimes never to recover, or they grow strong in character, possessing their vessel in honor and sanctification.

Girls are not initially possessed of sexual drive, but their desires for romance and their God-given need to be treasured and possessed by a man renders them vulnerable to the predatory conniving of immoral males. Girls can too easily become junkies for male attention, selling themselves cheap to get it. Girls in unhappy homes are the quickest to jump ship into the first male arms directed toward them.

I can understand why many parents want to isolate their children and save them from their vulnerability in this area, but you cannot isolate them from their imaginations and passions. It is extremely helpful if, when your children reach this age, they are greatly occupied with other things. If a boy is engaged in hard work and hard play, he will expend much of his testosterone in that manner. "An idle mind is the devil's workshop," is not an idle statement, but an idle body is the devil's toy as well.

THE KEY

We are addressing the vital issue of providing a safe social life for your teenagers. Here is the delicate key: You can inoculate them against runaway passions by controlled injections of a supervised social life. Children jump ship when they think their most pressing needs cannot be met on the present course of their voyage. If you continually isolate your boys on a ship with no exposure to girls, they will eventually go overboard, and once they do, you no longer have a say in the way they seek fulfillment. So, you must provide a social life that promises a strong expectancy of future fulfillment in this area. Teenagers are more likely to be patient if they can see that their ship is part of a fleet that will occasionally rendezvous in port with other ships carrying handsome young men and beautiful girls just waiting to be swept away.

In most cases, your children will marry someone from the circle in which they are raised. They will make their picks long before you ever imagined they were showing interest. Although they may change their minds several times, they will always have someone in their imaginations as a suitable future mate. Even if eventually they marry someone from outside their common social circle, your boys' ideas of what they like in a girl will have been formed from their early contacts (which you provided) with thirteen-, fourteen-, and fifteen-year-old girls, and they form them when they have just gone through puberty! And if you think you can replace this natural, God-given, God-ordered drive with teaching them Bible principles, you are off your religious rocker! But, we will talk about biblical admonition and character building later.

COMMUNITY

Ideally, your family should be part of a community of like-minded families who share the same biblical values and worldview. If your sixteen-year-old can look around and see a young woman whom he believes would make a great wife, he will hang around on your ship, doing his chores and making the sacrifices necessary to wait out the opportunity to enter into a marriage relationship on grounds that are acceptable to the community. There it is. Read that sentence again. He will wait for the opportunity to enter into marriage on *grounds that are acceptable to the community. The community is a more certain, powerful, regulating factor than is the self-control of the kids involved*—more powerful than his own convictions. Even teenagers who are not saved and do not possess personal convictions will go along with community values if that is what it takes for them to attain the deepest desire of their hearts—or of their flesh.

If you want to almost guarantee that your children with not jump ship (other factors being equal), provide a community life that holds promise of suitable future mates. If your community is narrow and self-righteous, your kids may decide early that they do not want to live like this the rest of their lives, and they may make up their minds that they are not going to marry and live in your community circle. They will look over the railing at other passing ships that seem to be more sincere and friendly. Once kids leave the natural constraining factors of community, all that is left to control them is their own wisdom and self-control, which is usually not enough to keep teenagers, even "Christian" teenagers, from doing something foolish and regrettable.

EXPANDING COMMUNITY

When I speak of providing a community, I am not necessarily speaking of the traditional "small town," old friends and family, all in one accord, going to the same country church, and having picnics at the city park after listening to gospel music and a political speech. That would certainly be nice, but in most cases, such an idyllic environment is gone forever in America. In some areas it can be partially recovered, but only at great difficulty and sacrifice.

Your family may be part of a very small church and community, offering few possibilities for your teenage children to find mates. It is a ship-jumping waiting to happen unless you can enlarge the community and the pool of possible marriage partners for your children. If you are in this situation, you must give immediate attention to expanding your community. One way of doing that is to get out and travel with your fifteen- to eighteen-year-olds, visiting other families with kids of a suitable age. Start attending camp meetings or Bible conferences, any gathering of Christians of like values. Your family must stay loosely connected in a way that provides your budding adult children with hopes of finding suitable mates. Seeing other families with possible mates, even once or twice a year, can be enough to give your young dreamers hope. When teenagers start dreaming of a particular mate, it creates a stabilizing influence in their lives. They will now have strong incentive to preserve their virtue for one whom they feel is worthy of nothing less.

There is a popular teaching that you should just tell your children to be patient, and God will bring into their life the one person created in heaven to be their mate. For a few very dedicated kids, who have committed their lives to serving God on the mission field or in some full-time capacity, this is doubtless true, and it will be enough to gain their trust and cause them to patiently wait. But, the average kid who has never experienced a deep walk of faith is not going to somehow have faith in this one area and just sit around until he is thirty years old waiting for that one special female to fall out of heaven into his arms.

We receive many letters like a recent one where a 28-year-old daughter has jumped ship and married an older divorced man with a smeared past and three children. As she was getting older, she saw the small pool of "possibles" dwindling away to nothing. She lost hope and needed love. She foolishly rejected her captain and her family, and threw herself to the sharks rather than continue on a lonely, hopeless voyage leading to old maid island. Older children and young adults must have a tangible, visible hope, one with a social life that provides potential mates of the same caliber as themselves.

I know that kids should exercise more self-restraint, that they should be more patient, and that they should listen to the counsel of their parents and their church elders. I also agree that they should be wise and spiritual and seek God's will first and foremost—but few do, whereas virtually all of them will eventually marry. Don't risk throwing your children away by setting the marriage standard so high that they despair of reaching it. You are making a grave mistake if you fail to provide for the possibility that your teenage children may not be spiritual, discerning giants. They may just end up marrying an acquaintance—one whom you provide, or one they meet at the video store.

God has chosen you as the captain of your ship. You are authorized to command your crew, but remember that many a voyage has ended with a very disheartened crew abandoning ship, or worse, in mutiny. Provide community for your children. Don't fail in this one last task you are commanded to carry out: providing adequate community for them so that you can happily send them ashore to produce Godly seed. Give them hope, and they will stick it out until you have safely delivered them to a lifemate worthy of the time and prayer you have invested in them.

CITY DWELLERS

If you live in an apartment in a big city, you can still provide community, but it will certainly not happen by default. It will take wise judgment and careful control. You must actively seek out others of like faith and convictions and create an association with them. In the city, you are not likely to find a church that provides a proper community life for your children. A church receives anyone and everyone who chooses to come through the door, as it rightly should. But to have a proper community for your teenage children, you must exercise your freedom not to associate with some families. You must pick and choose with wisdom. If you are a pushover, welcoming into your home all who would seek your association, you might as well throw your children to the dogs, for they are prone to adopt the worst influences you allow into their lives. If you can't judge between right and wrong and don't exhibit the courage to flee the company of evildoers, your children are in danger from your weak-kneed attitude. Learn to say "no" to companying with ungodly people, and mean it! Use the word, "No!" in ways that cannot be mistaken for, "Maybe some other time."

"No we don't want to go there."

"No, my children are being saved for something better."

"No, that is not our idea of fun."

"No, I think it would be better if our families did not mix; we have convictions that your children don't seem to share."

Will they call you "hypocrites, self-righteous, isolationists"? Yes, they will, and things a whole lot worse. But when you live in Sodom (any city in America), you will either let the popular trend be your guide, or you will set your own agenda and enforce it, no matter whose feelings get hurt. To select a righteous community of true believers out of your church or your city and guard its borders is not an easy task, but I know many families who have been successful at it. If a deadly virus were to sweep through the world, no one would fault you for quarantining your family. How much more deadly is the disease of sin that so infects the world today! Just make sure that your family "quarantine" shares its isolation with enough families so that it does not feel like isolation to the children. The point is not to cease having a social life, but to build your social life around your own worldview. There are families out there who are part of God's remnant, just like you.

CHAPTER 5

CHARACTER BUILDING

One of our readers wrote to our children, asking them to answer the question, "What did your daddy do that equipped you to overcome the world?" Here is the answer of our daughter, Rebekah.

SAFEGUARDING YOUR CHILDREN

Rebekah Joy (Pearl) Anast

Dad's reaction and openness about sin, and God's hatred of sin gave us assurance in dealing with the world when Dad wasn't around. One day when I was eight years old, I went down to the mailbox to get the mail. Lying in the grass near the mailbox was a magazine with a solid white cover. I assumed some of our mail had escaped the mailman and went over to pick it up. The magazine fell open in the middle, and for about three seconds I stared in amazed horror at the hard porn in front of me. A dozen conversations and statements that my Dad had made about such things came rushing to my mind.

I recall, once during a trip to Memphis with our family, on a downtown street, I saw a half-dressed woman being jerked around and slapped by a man in a pink suit.

"She's a prostitute," Dad told us. "He's a pimp—her handler. She works for him, selling her body to lascivious men who will burn in hell, so that she can continue to buy drugs to satisfy her addiction. God hates prostitution and pornography, kids. It destroys lives and families." We kids stared in horror at the man and woman who were now stumbling into a building with neon signs and blacked out windows.

"Do you know what pornography is?" Dad persisted. We stared at him, still shaken by what we had just seen. "It is photographs of naked men and women... and other things I won't even tell you about."

"Why do those women let people take pictures of them when they are naked?" we asked.

"Most of those women were molested when they were kids, by their uncles, their brothers, friends, or even by complete strangers. They have no sense of self-value now. They feel worthless, and so they don't guard their bodies. Instead, they sell their bodies for money to other worthless men who are molesting other women and girls." We all swallowed hard and shuddered.

"God hates this kind of sin so much, that when the children of Israel went into Canaan, he told Joshua to kill every man, woman, and child because they had all been involved in sexual sins. God says that it is better for a man to have a big wheat-grinding stone tied around his neck and be thrown into the sea to drown than to face the wrath of God that will come on him if he messes with little kids that way." We all nodded. It would be a just retribution for such an evil person.

"Whenever you see pornography, kids, I want you to turn away from it – don't look at it, because it will stay in your mind and bother you for years. Wad it up and burn it, or throw it away so no one else will ever see it. And don't trust anybody. If an uncle or cousin wants to talk to you about this kind of stuff—or touch you—I want you to scream at the top of your voice, and run away and tell on them. Don't be polite or wait to see if he's really a bad guy or not. The first minute you feel as though something is wrong, run away from that person…" Dad went on to give us detailed instructions about protecting ourselves and our minds. All of this came to my memory the moment that pornography magazine fell open in my eight-year-old hands. Even though I had never seen pornography before, I instantly knew what it was. A righteous indignation swelled up inside of me, and I crumpled the magazine up as small as I could get it and carried it home. I took it straight to Dad and told him about it. We set it on fire, and I felt a grim satisfaction for having destroyed one small piece of evil in my world.

When my brothers were ten and twelve years old, they found pornography stapled to the trees in the woods where some filthy hunter had left it for the Amish kids to find. My brothers reacted the same way I had. They turned their backs and approached each tree with their backs to it, pulled down the pages and wadded them up into tight balls, stuffed them in their backpacks and brought them home to burn.

I have often wondered what our reaction to pornography would have been if Dad had never told us about it. What if we hadn't known what kind of people create it and use it, and what God thinks about it? He even told us what to do WHEN we ran into it. . .not IF! Dad knew the world was so corrupt that there was no way he could shield us entirely. So he equipped us to handle the corruption ourselves. If I had never heard of pornography that day when I picked up the magazine, I think my own shocked curiosity would have led me to turn the pages and begin the searing of my conscience. Then, my sense of guilt would have kept me from telling my parents what I had found. And what would I have done with the magazine? Hidden it? Shared it with my brothers? I don't know. But the truth and knowledge I held that day ensured my freedom and safety. I thank God so much for what Dad did for us!

When I was 14 years old, we (my brothers and I) were swimming in the creek with our neighbors. They had three boys the same ages as we were: 14, 12, and 10 years of age. A perverted looking local drove by our swimming hole repeatedly, leering out the window at us. My brother Gabe made a comment about his probably being a queer. The 14-year-old friend looked curious and asked, "What's a queer?"

My brother replied, "You know – a faggot." The boy shook his head in confusion. Gabe said, "A homosexual." Still not understanding, the 14-year-old, homeschooled neighbor boy just shook his head. Gabe laughed, sure that his friend was playing dumb.

"Come on! You've got to know what a queer is. You know, guys that mess with other guys or boys. Perverts!"

To this day I can remember the look on the other boy's face. It was NOT a look of surprise and curiosity. It was a look that said, *"There's a word for it? You know about that? Do other people know about it? Do you know…?"* I felt sorry for our friend that day. I wondered what experiences he had run into—unprepared and unwarned.

Many times as a child I remember standing at Dad's side when he would go into a gas station to prepay fuel. If the station carried pornography, Dad would scrape his money back off of the counter and tell the cashier that he could not buy gas there because he just noticed they promoted rape and child molestation. The cashier would look shocked, and Dad would point at the porn magazines behind him. The cashier ALWAYS looked guilty and ashamed. He would glance at us kids; we would all be looking at him with suspicious shock (are you a child molester???) before we turned and walked out. These incidents burned a firm and lasting impression into us. Dad's reaction and openness about sin, and God's hatred of sin gave us assurance in dealing with the world when Dad wasn't around.

KNOWING GOOD AND EVIL—FROM GOD'S PERSPECTIVE OF GOOD

Our parents also made sure we understood the difference between righteous sexuality and evil sexuality. There was a clear distinction in our minds. When we were very small, Dad candidly explained that God created all beings, male and female, for pleasure and reproduction. God created sex to be pure and holy between one man and one woman, who would eventually be Mommy and Daddy to a whole passel of kids. There wasn't supposed to be any confusion or shame in that relationship. It was intended by God to be whole, functional, and happy.

When our dogs were mating, Dad called us outside to see what they were doing, then told us to go back inside and give them some privacy. Inside, at the kitchen table, he sat down with some paper and a pen and drew a picture for us of sperm swimming up a canal to an egg. He gave us a thorough, practical explanation of reproduction. We were 8, 6, 4, and 2 years old.

I was so excited about the miracle of the whole process, that when my cousin came over later in the day (she was 9 years old), I got out Dad's diagram and tried to tell her what he had told us. Fortunately, I couldn't remember the exact names of parts, and went to ask Mom. She hastily took the paper from me and said that it was up to my cousin's parents to tell her about all that stuff, and that I wasn't supposed to talk about it outside the family. Later on, Dad explained to me with more detail that the facts of life is a subject that just isn't discussed in public, even though it isn't shameful. I didn't understand fully, but I knew I could take his word for it.

Our parents gave us a happy understanding of marriage by letting us see them hug, kiss, and enjoy each other's company. They never gave us the specifics of sex, but often assured us that marriage was great and that God had someone wonderful in store for each of us if we stayed pure and walked in righteousness until it was time to get married. This great example, contrasted so clearly with occasional glimpses of the ugliness of sin, and made it easy for me to make up my mind to wait for the best man for me.

Many parents write us saying that they are trying to protect their children's innocence. They don't want them to know about the evil in the world. I understand their concern. It is a sad thing that we live in a world where evil has such free reign, where child porn is available to anyone who wants to access it. It is sickening. I hope the Lord returns for us soon and breaks the teeth of the ungodly before He casts them into the lake of fire, where they will be in torment for eternity. But the truth is, children are going to come across the reality of our corrupt society one way or another. They will either hear it from a twisted pervert, another clueless kid who is making poor guesses and choices, Hollywood, a book, the Internet, or... maybe even from you. Which source do you want them to get it from first? Dad made sure he was the first to tell us life's secrets; he made sure his information was the most thorough and complete; and he made sure we knew everything from the standpoint of good, rather than evil.

TO PARENTS

I know a girl who is twenty years old and still a virgin. She is beautiful, outgoing, and smart. There is a constant stream of guys vying for her attention. She smiles at them and shakes her head, "no," when they ask her to go out with them. "I'm not ready to get married yet," she tells them. I once heard her telling some other young people that when she meets the man she thinks might be the one, and he asks her out, she is going to bring her family along on their first date as a surprise. She has two sisters and two brothers and a very lively mom and dad. If he is still interested after that first date with her very rowdy family, she says she'll consider him. By now you may have a mental image of a very spiritual homeschooled girl with long hair and a denim jumper, plus a solid history of innocence. Not so. This girl was raised in an unbelieving family until she was ten years old. Her dad was an alcoholic before he got saved. She went to public school (bad public schools) from kindergarten through high school. Her parents impose no rules of clothing, music, dating, or anything at all, really! She can come and go as she likes, and date whomever she likes. But she never has. Why? She is walking after the Spirit of God and her parents, and not after a list of rules.

From the day her parents got saved, they began to seek God with their whole heart. They didn't seek religion. Not Church. Not even the Bible. Just God, and God alone. They laid aside their vices completely to follow Him. They seek him daily on their knees, and minister day and night to the people around them. They are not trying to balance their Christianity and their comfort. They seek to please God, not themselves. Their home is full of needy people all the time, people I wouldn't want my kids to be around. This girl saw the change in her parents.

She has watched their 100% sincerity for ten years now. She has seen the fruit of that dedication. She wants it. Rules would never have persuaded her to turn away from the world. Their love for God did.

Children will usually follow the spirit of their parents. I have met a few young people who have heroically decided to be godly and real, despite their parents; but this is the exception, not the rule. The father doesn't have to be a porno freak for the son to get involved in it. All he has to do is sit with his arm around his wife at church and then show disregard for her at home. The mother doesn't have to be a prostitute for her daughter to take that road; all she has to do is show scorn for her husband and disobey his requests. This hypocrisy will communicate to the children that there are two rules of law in the universe: pleasing the crowd, and pleasing yourself. They'll grow up believing that if they can maintain a religious front at church, what goes on at home is their own business. God is actually out of the picture for such a family.

Any measure at all of hypocrisy will undermine the moral strength of your children. Absolute consistency on every level will strengthen and enable them to be even greater than you are. Consistency communicates that God is to be feared; inconsistency communicates that God is only "let's pretend." It says, "God can be turned off."

DAD, ARE YOU KEEPING THE WORLD OUT?
(Rebekah Pearl Anast)

The world used to be out there on the perimeters of our lives. It was possible to shut ourselves away and remain untouched by the filth we heard rumors of. In order to be a porno freak, men had to drive to an adult bookstore, and go inside to buy a magazine from a nasty looking character they would never want to be associated with. Now, pornography barges into our sight on billboards, commercials, and web pages. Whether you are looking for it or not, it will find you.

The most amazing thing about the rise of pornography on the internet is not how many children have gotten involved, but how many "mature, responsible people" went off the deep end. People who thought they were safe in their own righteousness have fallen into immorality. No Greater Joy receives letters from pastors, elders, and fathers who have professed Christianity for years but are now in the tangle of pornography. They were unprepared for temptation in their own home. They never learned to stand and fight and resist the Devil.

Shutting evil out of your life is not really an act of righteousness. Just about the time believers (and stoic, clean-living non-believers) learn to deal with pornography on the web, some greater and more insidious evil will be introduced by the world at large. The answer is something more aggressive and more fundamental! The answer is to believe the gospel, the reality of your sanctification, and that you are dead to sin and alive unto God. In this stand of faith you will worship God in the Spirit and have no confidence in the flesh. You will walk after the Spirit and thus not fulfill the lust of the flesh. You will be free from sin right down to the most secret and fundamental part of your being. When Paul wrote Romans and told the believers that they should "through the Spirit… mortify the deeds of the body," he wasn't talking about some Sunday school rules that they should abide by. Half-baked churchianity is never enough to overcome the world. If you are not overcoming sin, you need to listen to my Dad's audio series called "Sin No More."

Even the most secluded and conservative families will be assaulted. Shutting out as much evil as you can is your God-given duty to your children, but you will never be able to shut it all out. On top of that, you cannot make your children pure by insulating and isolating their circumstances. You must train, teach, and prepare their minds to respond to the Spirit of God.

TO THE YOUTH *(Beka)*

You are the future. I won't tell you that waiting for your mate isn't hard. It is. I have wondered a million times why God gave teenagers such powerful, raging hormones. Why couldn't He have placed that hormonal curse on the old folks that have all the patience and discipline in the world? It's hard just to keep your thoughts straight, sometimes. But if you knew what is waiting for you... if you only knew how good it could be! You would never accept a toy car in the place of a real, shiny red Porsche.

Don't listen to the disillusioned and bitter couples who talk about how hard marriage is, struggling to get along and trying to make it work. If they talk like that, you can bet they messed up somewhere in the past and have no idea what marriage was intended to be. They think their broken product is the way all marriages are constituted. They are wrong. Out of dozens of marriages (good marriages, but not trouble free), we know of only three that came from pure pasts on both sides, neither of them bringing into the marriage any regrets or moral down-falls. Those three marriages were fantastic from the start.

The Bible says, "Be not deceived, God is not mocked; whatsoever a man soweth, that shall he also reap." If you sow trouble with your flesh before marriage, you'll reap trouble later on. If you sow purity – oh, yes! It can be sooooooooooo good! Take it from us (my husband and I): a pure youth makes for a fantastic marriage, without regrets, without heartache, and without fear. Neither one of us has had second thoughts, and we never will. Be assured: waiting is so worth it!

A few weeks after I married Gabe, he told me something funny. He said one of the things he most valued about me was that I wasn't an "accidental" virgin. He said he had met conservative homeschooled youth from a dozen families who were virgins just by happenstance. They hadn't personally made a choice to be pure. The parents had made that choice for them—which is good—but the kids had never made that choice for themselves. He said there was no telling how many of them would have given away their virginity if they had been placed in new circumstances and allowed to do whatever they pleased. Have you made a choice yet? Are you doing as much as you can get away with in the confines of your parents' ruling, or are you personally walking after the Spirit of God? Do your convictions change with the crowd you're in, or do you know who you are?

Even the Bible college for missionary kids that I attended in 1992 taught a watered-down form of righteousness for the single person. They discussed whether or not dating, holding hands, kissing, sexual deviances, etc., were okay. Everyone had different standards. One day a frustrated student called out, "Why didn't God just tell us what we ought to do? Why didn't He just give us a list of dos and don'ts?" The professor couldn't answer him. At that time, I didn't know the answer either. I felt just like that student. Why couldn't there be a list of rules to go by? But he gave us something much better—his most HOLY Spirit.

BACK TO MIKE

You just read the personal testimony of my daughter Rebekah. As I write this, I am almost 63 years old. It is hard to remember all the things I did and the manner in which I admonished my children in spiritual things. But just yesterday, I had a young man, sixteen years old, come to work with me for the day. He is a fine believer, but I knew little of him. After the day's work, I realized that I took every opportunity to casually influence his thinking and worldview. I gave him a dozen warnings about everything from controlling sexual impulses to the need to do one's duty and not be lazy. I also schooled him in everything from how to pick up a concrete block without hurting your back to how to keep from getting hurt when working around big equipment. I spoke of the evils of sugar in your diet and of the evils of dishonesty.

When I made a mistake in work that set us back a couple of hours, I noticed that he watched to see if I would get mad. While it was happening, I was conscious of his watching and knew that my reaction was going to be more influential than all the words I spoke that day. I realized later that I put as much energy into tutoring him in life and responsibility as I did into work. None of this was by design. I was not following some principles of mentoring. I just related to him as my heart and mind dictated, just as I had related to my children when they were growing up. The experience with this young man unconsciously thrust me back into that role. I realize that I feel the need and have a desire to steer young people in the right direction. It is not a "time out from routine events." Teaching is life itself.

It brought to mind the way I taught my children as they were coming up from infancy. There was no time when I wasn't teaching: Every action, every word, all of life was teaching.

CHAPTER 6

<hr />

BIBLICAL ADMONITION
(Michael Pearl)

What was different about Abraham that God should chose him to be both the progenitor of Israel and the father of all who believe? As a general rule, all God's blessings are based purely on grace, with no mention of any merit in the man. But Abraham is one of the rare exceptions. When God came in angelic form to visit him with the announcement that his wife Sarah was going to conceive, he said to the angel that accompanied him, "For I know him, that he will command his children and his household after him, and they shall keep the way of the LORD, to do justice and judgment; that the LORD may bring upon Abraham that which he hath spoken of him" (Genesis 18:19). God had confidence that Abraham would transmit his faith to his children for generations to come.

Are you planting your faith so deep in your children that they will pass it on for generations to come? Many parents are trying very hard to do so but are failing, because what they are trying to communicate is religion, rather than life. Second generation religion is as useless as food that has already been eaten. Life is dynamic, self-sustaining, adaptable, energetic, creative, and it is freedom in the extreme.

Life never rests. It has no down time. It can never be shelved. Life is not a series of concepts that one must keep organized and properly apply. Life comes from our deepest self within—from our spirits, where the Holy Spirit resides. The Bible says of Jesus, "In him was life."

It has been, it seems, a long time since we had young children and were engaged in admonishing them—communicating life. All the little details, many of which our daughter Rebekah recounted, have faded in my memory. But when I spend any time with young kids, the fountain is opened, and I remember the driving force that was the catalyst for all that I communicated to my children. As I observe myself, I realize that I am compelled by a consuming desire to mold children into righteousness while they are still pliable. I want to train them to be hard working, intelligent, well-informed, capable human beings, who love God and their neighbors. I am conscious of the value of every moment in their lives. I see them as adults, as eternal souls who are becoming something, be it good or bad, for eternity. I must do what I can to turn their hearts in the right direction. I must do it now, for this moment is more valuable than all moments past, and it is the foundation of all future moments. This very minute may be a turning point in a child's life. Now is the time. Not tomorrow. I **must** invest myself in them. I cannot do otherwise. Of all the things in my life clamoring for attention, what can be of more value?

I must confess that I do not know how to admonish you to the same end. Just the other day a man told me that he didn't love his fifth child—not much more than a toddler. I didn't know what to say. How do you tell a man to care deeply? I feel the same helplessness trying to tell you how to *feel* regarding admonishing your children. Religion can perform the acts of love, but only life loves all the time, in the good times and the bad, when the other is lovely and when they are not. Only life stirs itself through bone weariness and the clamoring of daily duty to invest itself in developing children. I take Jesus as my model, who rebuked his disciples when they tried to prevent the children from disturbing him. I can do no less.

God revealed to Israel that the great need of the family was to "turn the heart of the fathers to the children, and the heart of the children to their fathers, lest I come and smite the earth with a curse" (Malachi 4:5-6). That was the ministry of John the Baptist. It will also be the ministry of two witnesses during the Tribulation. It is forever the need of the family—to turn the hearts of the fathers to their children, which will result in the hearts of the children being turned to their fathers. When fathers have the hearts of their children there will be no ship jumping.

BIBLE DOCTRINE

I do not know how to turn your heart to your children, but as I reflect on this subject, I believe that the thing that turned my heart in that direction was my awareness of eternity. Knowledge of the Bible (of God) imparts an accurate perspective on reality. I do believe that cold hearts can be stirred and indifference can rise to passionate caring when one is immersed in Bible knowledge. I do not speak of catechisms and dogmatic theology, but a simple knowledge of the Bible stories from Genesis to Revelation— a knowledge that sees God at work in history, then and now.

To walk after the spirit and not after the flesh is the foundation of sound parenting. A father who worships God continuously will have the heart of his children. I am not talking about walking around in a trance-like state of piety, but of constantly appreciating the glory of God and deferring to his will in all things. Worship is not something you do once a week with a musical background in a dimly lit auditorium, guided by a group of professional soul stimulators. Worship is what a bricklayer does when he thanks God for the strength of his hands. Worship is what a tax assessor does in stalled traffic on the interstate when he recalls the 66th chapter of Isaiah and smiles to himself in anticipation of seeing the reality some-day. Worship is stepping outside for a moment and feeling the breath of God on your face and listening to the trees clap their hands in praise to God. Worship is being thankful for the mercy of God and accessing his grace daily. A worshiper of God will speak of him to sinners and to those in need.

The father whose heart is turned to God will turn that same heart toward his children.

The son or daughter of a worshiper of God will become a worshiper as well.

TEACHING THE BIBLE TO YOUR CHILDREN

I know that you can point to one or more families who taught their children the Bible, and saw them jump ship any-how. I hate to sound like the siren that screeches every Satur-day at noon down here in the Southern towns, but I must say it again; there is a difference between teaching the Bible as a religious book and teaching it as historical truth. Religion is the Devil's substitute for life. Religious teaching is the Devil's alternative to personal knowledge of God. Knowledge of dog-matic theology is a substitute for knowing the will and way of God in one's daily life.

So many religious parents employ the Bible *against* their children as a means of intimidating them into being "good" kids. Others use it as a resource from which to derive sound, workable principles that will guide them to a life of success and happiness, which is nothing more than humanism wearing religious vestments. Some use it as inspiration to strengthen or fortify themselves—their psychological vitamins. Still others read it as they would poetry or wise proverbs—enter Shakespeare and Tennyson. I could go on. There are a thousand ways to render the Bible feeble.

The correct use of the Bible is to read it as history. It obviously makes a difference how you view it when you read it. One can be inspired by a fictional story that celebrates bravery or triumph. One can find encouragement and guidance through any wise proverbs or sound psychological utterance, but only history is reality—a guide for our future. The Bible is a book written by God. It is his account of history—His-Story. It reveals the nature and will of God in simple historical accounts. The Bible is not about "God speaking to me" at this moment. It is about God having revealed himself on the stage of human history.

CHRONOLOGICAL REVELATION

Why did God wait 4,000 years after the fall of Adam to send Christ into the world? Why did he take so much time with Abraham, Moses, and the children of Israel? Because man can only understand God in history, in events. To understand who God is, it took 4,000 years of God's relating to man about the good and the bad, in his blessings and in his cursings, in the giving of the law and in God's response when they broke it. God made a powerful statement about who he is when he destroyed the world in Noah's day, and again when the destroyed the Sodomites with fire. We see a wonderful plan of God in his promises and blessings to Abraham and his descendants. His prophecies established once and for all that he is omnipotent, controlling the very calendar of events down to the end times. The law tells us that God is narrow-minded about sin and righteousness. The sacrifices tell us that there is forgiveness, but only in substitution and atonement. "But when the fulness of the time was come, God sent forth his Son, made of a woman, made under the law, to redeem them that were under the law, that we might receive the adoption of sons" (Galatians 4:4-5). That "fulness of time" was 4,000 years of history.

God told his story in history. Not in principles and concepts, but in history. Today, we learn about God, just as the Jews did, by recounting that history. The short of it is, God has given you a very simple means of acquainting your children with God. Read the Bible to them. Tell the stories over and over again. "Whom shall he teach knowledge? and whom shall he make to understand doctrine? *them that are* weaned from the milk, *and* drawn from the breasts. For precept *must* be upon precept, precept upon precept; line upon line, line upon line; here a little, *and* there a little" (Isaiah 28:9-10). Start them off on Bible stories when they are still nursing.

Don't fall into the trap of only telling kids' versions of David and Goliath and Jonah and the whale. Never tell the Bible stories with a Santa Claus levity. Get them a talking animal book if you want to entertain them with nonsense. A good test as to whether or not a Bible story is appropriate for kids is to ask yourself if it is still meaningful to you. If you remove a Bible story so far from the context that it is just cute, you are denigrating God's word. Don't rely on the highlight stories that are found in children's Bible story books. Read the Bible through, cover to cover, and tell them what you read. Don't wait for "devotional" time. It is much better to tell the stories during your daily routine, as they are appropriate to the moment. By the time your kids are ten years old, they should know the basic theme of the entire Bible from beginning to end.

Paul reveals the manner in which the Bible stories should be employed when he addressed the Corinthians: "Neither murmur ye, as some of them also murmured, and were destroyed of the destroyer. Now all these things happened unto them for ensamples: and they are written for our admonition, upon whom the ends of the world are come" (1 Corinthians 10:10-11). In instructing them not to murmur (complain), he reminds them of how God brought judgment on Israel for complaining. He then tells us that these things were written down as a means of instructing us in the will of God.

When you and your children are thoroughly acquainted with the Bible stories, you can instruct them in a matter of seconds by simply referring to one of the historical events. "Children, remember what happened to the children of Israel when they committed fornication: God killed three thousand of them in one day." One of my favorites was, "Kids, be careful what you eat; remember how Lefty got Fatty; the knife went in up to the hilt, and they didn't even know he had been stabbed." You are missing a world of wealth—4000 years of history—if your family is not acquainted with the Bible stories.

The Bible is clear, "The fear of the Lord is the beginning of wisdom" (Psalm 111:10). Also, "The fear of the LORD *is* the beginning of knowledge" (Proverbs 1:7). "The fear of the LORD tendeth to life" (Proverbs 19:23). Many other great virtues are attributed to the fear of the Lord. To instill a wholesome fear of God in your children is a gift most precious. That can only be done one of two ways. Either they personally witness or experience great judgments, or they read about such judgments in the Bible and believe it. We made sure that our children got it with both barrels. We spoke often of Bible stories, and we spoke of God's judgments in the lives of people with whom they were acquainted. They saw professing Christians disobey God and suffer great chastisements. We took every opportunity to draw their attention to God working in our own lives and the lives of those around us. God nearly killed me one time for disobeying. When I was finally able, I spoke of it publicly and made sure everyone knew that God had chastened me nearly unto death. It increased my fear of God, and theirs as well.

"The fear of the Lord tendeth to life." The Bible is a much easier way to learn the fear of God. It is God's gift, the only record of his work in the human race for 4,000 years.

CHAPTER 7

WHAT TO DO WHEN YOUR CHILD
HAS JUMPED SHIP

Today, children are divorcing their parents—leaving home before their time, rejecting authority, and turning their backs on their parents' culture. We have been calling it "jumping ship." Divorce is more accurate. Divorce produces self-doubt on the one hand, and blame on the other. Blame usually prevails. It's more comfortable.

You had no idea that it would come to this. When your son was about ten years old, you noticed that he didn't seem to enjoy your presence. You were a source of irritation. It was as if he wanted to say something, but would never come out with it. He turned away in frustration and sought friendship outside the home. Occasionally, he would explode in anger, and of all things, blaming you. You remember him blurting out, "You don't understand!" It carried a tone of accusation. It may have gotten to the point where he accused you of not caring. You hoped it was just a stage that he would grow out of, but he sank deeper into his aloneness. Then one day, when he was old enough and had the resources, he just left. There was anger; words thrown around like bullets; bombs of accusation were dropped; it turned into a word war of vengeance, all the time not believing that it could actually happen. But it did. And you knew failure as you have never known it before. I have known parents who, upon losing their first child, just gave up on the whole family, and they all fragmented and broke up like an airplane that had lost its wings.

We are now going to talk about what to do if your kid has jumped ship. How should you respond? Is it too late? Is all lost, or is there still hope, still a way? In every human conflict, two thirds of a correct response amounts to not doing what you shouldn't. If we humans could just turn off and shut down— do nothing—,we would be two thirds of the way to recovery. Most likely, however, your mouth is what dug the pit in the first place, so be warned that it is now your mouth that will throw vile dirt into the face of your estranged child. If you don't bridle your tongue, your religion is vain (James 1:26), for the tongue is a fire that is set on fire by hell itself (James 3:5-6). The same mouth cannot praise God at church and curse your son at home (James 3:10).

There is nothing that more readily induces us to anger than having our failures talk back to us. Let's face it. It is your own loss that causes you anger—loss of peace, loss of control, loss of prestige and respect, loss of your "perfect" life. "How could you do this TO ME after all I have done for you?" Blame.

As sinners, we tend to respond to criticism and rejection with anger. We take it as an attack upon our undeserving person. Fight back! Stand up for our rights. SMASH! You hurt me. There, I hurt you more. You will be sorry! You will come back crawling and begging for forgiveness. "I, your majesty, await your humble apology, and then perhaps my wrath will be appeased." Hell hath enlarged itself. Just remembering we are humans—sons of Adam—ought to humble us. Pride is the fuel of hell's fire, and each of us is an unlimited source of combustion.

It is the kid's fault, right? Beware of blame. It is the first refuge of the guilty. Blame is the end of creativity. It is a dead-end road, traveled only for the dark and lonely pleasure it gives. When you blame, you surrender hope of changing things, because you lay all the responsibility upon a moral agent over whom you admittedly have no control. Blame affords you the opportunity to play God for a little while—a one-sided god who sits to judge without mercy. Satan loves the spirit of blame. It comes in a dark cloud that permits no mercy and refuses insight. Blame is tunnel vision that excludes any positive perspective and magnifies fault to the criminal level. Blame is the way to cook down disappointment until it turns to thick hate. Blame is the solace of devils and their finishing touch on all sin and human failure. To go there is to return with nothing but bitterness and the satisfaction of knowing it was "not your fault." But the end is the same, no matter whose fault it was.

It happened on your watch. Your kid didn't come into the world emotionally broken and angry. So far, all I have done is inform you that all your responses have exacerbated the problem. This has not been to punish you, but to make you stop the blaming. Your first step to recovery must be to get your own heart right with God. I want you to stop digging the pit deeper. I have been functioning as a prophet, calling you to repentance. It is the only starting place.

You must become what you want your child to become, if you would bring him to repentance. You must become a person of joy, peace, and love. You must know God and love him. You must be disciplined and holy in your own personal life. You must tend to your marriage so that it becomes the envy of all who know you well.

RULE ONE: ACCEPT YOUR SON'S DECISION TO DIVORCE YOU.

It is done. There is no going back. Stop treating him as a child to be intimidated. Never again accuse or blame him. Never mention that you are hurt. Act as if his leaving was a natural occurrence that had your approval. This will be impossible for you if you are carrying a grudge, a desire to hurt or to punish. When your heart is truly set on the future, on making the best of the present circumstances, you will lay down all of the past and relate to your son as if he were a lonely and needy kid whom you just met and are moved to bring hope and joy to his life. If the issue is your feelings and your justification, you will eventually drop a bitter or accusing word, and he will shake you off like mud between his fingers. This is the starting place for any recovery that may yet be possible. Your son is not a prodigal son. You have been a prodigal father! So, skip any talk of his being to blame. If you don't, you will be immersing your parental failure in concrete.

RULE TWO: GIVE UP ALL PERCEIVED PARENTAL RIGHTS AND AUTHORITY.

Don't demand that he come back and meet you on a parent-son foundation. Accept the fact that you must now earn the right to have even a small part in his life, and that by his invitation only. Just as you would carefully approach a co-worker at the office whom you perceive has been wounded and hurt by life, exercising all respect and patience, so you must approach your son. Don't think in terms of him breaking down and coming back as your little boy, admitting his guilt and inadequacies, begging your advice, and putting his messed-up life in your hands. It will never happen.

We have listed only two rules so far and already it is too much for most wounded parents. You are arguing with me. There is no use going any further until you get these first two right.

RULE THREE: PRAY FOR YOUR SON.

Pray for him from God's perspective, until your heart breaks. When you see him as potential glory to God, and your prayers are no longer about you and your feelings of hurt, then God can have the freedom to begin moving in his life.

Your prayers will be wasted if you are thinking in terms of recovering your personal loss—of fixing your life. You can't truly pray until all anger, ambition, and blame are gone, because you would only be praying to "consume it upon your lusts."

RULE FOUR: MAINTAIN CONTACT ON A LEVEL THAT IS NOT SMOTHERING TO YOUR SON.

Be sensitive to his signals. It may take a cooling off period before he will admit you back into his circle. If he has been hurt very badly, he may seek to cut off all contact with you. If so, you must somehow communicate that you are not blaming him and that you are not going to ride his back; you must persuade him that you are going to respect his decision to divorce the family. Once he spends an hour or so with you and discovers that things are truly different, that you are relaxed, and that you have gotten off your high horse, he will lose some of his apprehension. When the time is right, invite him to a family outing, or to dinner. Don't badger him about "going to church." It didn't make much difference in the previous seventeen years he lived at home. Why would it matter now? Guard your lips, bite your tongue, and pray that God will totally change your heart toward this son, because if your heart is not right, your mouth will find a way to slip in some accusation or expression of hurt. And, should that happen, he won't stay around long enough to cast a shadow in your home.

RULE FIVE: OFFER ASSISTANCE AS IT IS APPROPRIATE.

You must pray for divine wisdom. You do not want to support a decadent lifestyle and facilitate any irresponsibility, but you will want to offer any assistance that leads to his assuming responsibility. Initially, when you have little to no contact at all, when mistrust is still in the air, you may offer to do his laundry, help with the shopping, loan him some pots and pans, and help him secure second-hand furniture. The whole family could offer to go over and paint his apartment. Any gesture that indicates your goodwill will cover a multitude of sins and ill will. You don't want to shield him from the realities of independence, but neither do you want him to be overpowered with responsibility to the point that he crashes and fails. You might think that the hard circumstances will force him to come home begging. Beware! He will see through your attitude. If he is forced to come home as a failure, nothing will be accomplished in the way of building relationships. If you can help him to succeed, the fellowship of accomplishment may so heal the relationship that he could want to come back home in a few weeks or months. But keep in mind that your goal is not to get him back home, and thereby prove that you were right and he was wrong. Your goal is to see a young man become a happy, successful man of God. You will probably find that you get along better with him away from "home." It may be that it will be better for him to remain independent. Some people are much easier to like from afar. And that works both ways.

RULE SIX: CULTIVATE FELLOWSHIP WITH YOUR PRODIGAL.

Read the parable of the Prodigal Son found in Luke 17. It so beautifully portrays the kind of heart you must have toward your son. If you find you are more like the older brother, don't expect the prodigal to come home. We fellowship with people we can trust with knowledge about us. To fellowship is to be vulnerable. When you care, and caring leads to giving, to bearing one another's burdens, there is fellowship.

It was lack of fellowship that caused your son to leave in the first place. If you disagree with that assessment, you have not yet repented. You are still blaming. Your son is not going to like you any more now than he did the day he fled the ugliness of your relationship with him at home. If you are as I described, I don't like you either. Your wife probably doesn't like you. What about the rest of the children? You already lost this one. What has changed to keep you from losing the rest? So, you have changed churches to get rid of the bad influence. You have gotten rid of the television and the video games. You have tightened up and are making sure the other children understand responsibility. But I hope you are not berating your departed son to the younger children in a belief that they will fear to take the path he has taken. I hope you are not storming around the house, locking doors like a man who just discovered that he has been burglarized, passing new rules and venting your anger. If so, say "good-bye" to the other children. Your departed son will want to "save" them from you as soon as he can.

This may still be a mystery to you, a big, tangled, unfathomable mess, but to me it is predictable. I can see right through you, and I am not that smart. You need to love God to the point that you break out in singing praises to Him. You need to walk after the Spirit so that you do not fulfill the lust of the flesh. You must become an attractive human being. Everyone is attracted to joy and creativity. You must be kind, affectionate, tender-hearted, forgiving one another. You must be merciful and long-suffering. You must be known to be disciplined and temperate.

You cannot have the sweet fruit of life if you don't plant the right seeds. Christian fruit comes from a Christian tree—from Christ!. Only the Holy Spirit can bear Spirit fruit. I am not being religious. I am not throwing these things in just to flavor my exhortation with a pious and spiritual-sounding speech. A Spirit-filled life is the ONLY hedge against jumping ship and divorce.

One way to gauge your spiritual condition before God is to download Bible teaching Free on our web site. You must listen to the entire Romans series. I am not selling you anything. It's FREE! We have received thousands of letters expressing joy and victory through the Word of God. Just thinking about you rejoicing in Christ Jesus makes me start liking you already. It will do the same for your prodigal son.

A SUCCESS STORY

Several years ago, a father sought my counsel on the dire conditions in his home. His teenage son was rebellious and ill-tempered, and it was rubbing off on the younger kids. The father knew that his son would leave the home just as soon as he felt that he could survive on his own. He did not want reconciliation and resisted all overtures to discussing the matter. He acted as if it was his parents' fault, but he never said anything specific. His short, rude retorts just revealed hurt and anger.

"What do I do?" the father asked.

I told him, "It is not about doing; it is about being—being

the kind of human person that your son can respect." The father readily admitted that "much" of the trouble was his fault, so he was willing to receive counsel and "DO" something to bring healing.

I told him to go home and inform his son that he has discovered that he has failed as a person and likewise as a father, and that the son's poor spirit is a result of having a lousy father. Tell the boy that you know it is too late to change things very much for him, but that you do not want the same unhappiness to continue in the younger children. Tell him that you need his help. Hand him a sheet of paper, and ask him to write down at least five things that father and mother could have done differently that would made home life better for the children.

Don't be surprised if he brushes you off and refuses to cooperate. Look at it from his perspective. Have you ever had a discussion with him about these issues that didn't end in further misunderstanding and anger? He thinks you are trying to get him to be vulnerable so you can attack him again. He is not going to want to stick his emotional hand out, only to get it whacked off again. Don't expect immediate participation. He has no hope. So give him a glimmer of hope. Don't blame or accuse. Over the next several days, demonstrate yourself to be a different person—a real person of kindness, self-discipline, patience, mercy and understanding. Love your wife. Create an enviable life. Enjoy the other children. Speak of your repentance to your friends. Let it be known that you are a repentant sinner, seeking to be a real Christian.

This can't be fanned. Your son is a good psychologist. He knows you better than you know yourself, because your ego deceives you. Prove that you are a new man, and so give your son hope that he can be a new son. If your son didn't respond favorably to your first request, in a few days to two weeks, again ask him to write down those things that you need to change that will prevent the other children from coming to the same bitterness that he now feels. Tell him that you are not going to read his responses in his presence, and that you are not going to come back and challenge him on any of them. He expects you to defend yourself and to turn his answers around so as to further incriminate him. Tell him that you are going to take his list to God and not argue them with him. Assure him that there are no "wrong" answers. What he feels, whether justified or not, is reality, his reality, the only reality that matters where your son is concerned.

When you prove yourself, and he comes to partially trust you, and when he senses just a little inkling of hope, he will write down his true feelings. Do with his list what you said you would. Take his responses to God, and ask him to reveal your heart condition to you and to change you from the inside out. Your son will watch you like a hawk to see what the impact is going to be.

What can you expect him to write down? What might he say? About ten years ago, in preparation for a large seminar in the Dallas, Forth Worth area, I sent a questionnaire to the pastor to give to the hundreds of young homeschoolers who would be in attendance. We first asked the children, "Are you satisfied with your home life, are you happy, or would you like to change some things about it?" Only one or two kids said they would not change anything. We then asked the kids who were not happy to write down three things that, if changed, would make them happy at home. We were shocked to see that nearly every one shared the same perspective on their first answer. In one way or another, they said, "If my mama and daddy just loved each other…or wouldn't fight all the time."

A prominent second answer was, "If my daddy wasn't so angry."

Quite a few said, "If my parents would listen to me," or "spend more time with me."

Some said, "If my parents weren't such hypocrites."

Hardly any of the kids recorded anything frivolous or self-centered.

Now, knowing what to expect, are you still willing to ask your teenager to critique you? Are you humbled enough by your failure to believe his answers? Are you willing to submit your whole life to God and experience a complete revival of love and discipleship with Jesus?

Let me say it again, your life cannot be segmented or partitioned. You cannot be a good parent while being a lousy husband or wife. You cannot be a successful family man while maintaining secret sin. Your sins in any area "will find you out", and you will see the ugly fruit in your children. You are one person, a whole person, and you must turn your whole life over to God completely. If you only give God half, your children only get half—the worst half.

Well, the man who approached me about his wayward son did go home and eventually gain his son's cooperation in making a list. The father experienced a revival within, and the son came to respect his father and mother in their renewed relationship. The entire family experienced healing and spiritual growth. We here at No Greater Joy Ministries have received thousands of letters from happy parents who have had their ashes turned into a river of joy.

When is it too late? If you are eighty years old and your son is sixty, it is not too late to restore respect. The same steps are still necessary. Hearts are the same at any age.

Many of you, my readers, are already formulating a letter to me, because you think you have unique circumstances that are not covered here. Don't send that letter until you can tell me that you are singing and rejoicing in Jesus Christ and are enjoying your spouse in a life of thanksgiving and praise. That kind of life will cause any ship jumper to swim back to your boat and ask to sign on for the rest of the voyage.

GABRIEL ANAST *(Michael Pearl's son-in-law)* SPEAKS TO YOUNG PEOPLE

God was actually specific. The word "fornication" in the Scriptures is sexual activity outside the confines of marriage. That means, any activity or thought that you pursue for sexual pleasure. This law of God allows for different standards for different people. A thirteen-year-old boy won't be able to look at or do things that a sixty-year-old lady could, with a clear conscience.

Sexual highs are meant to be enjoyed by one man and one woman in a context that is sacred and safe from the intrusion of other people. But in order for marriage to be holy, those who enter into it must themselves be holy.

Imagine a couple standing at the altar in their wedding finery. Both of them having slept around, more recently with each other. What does the "holy bonds of matrimony" mean to them? What privileged act of pleasure are they going to receive now that they are married? What *could have been* is now spoiled and gone. They have the same stolen goods they took before their vows, plus doubt, mistrust, and a nagging sense of discontentment and shame. There is no elation or joy in the perfect gift of physical union. There is no gift at all; only spoiled, stolen goods.

Sex is not just a pleasurable act of procreation. It is an act of kindness, care, and generosity. For a woman, it is like an act of worship; for a man, it is an act of joy in the blessings and gifts of his wife. Those highs are righteous, glorious, and pure. God gave us these intense feelings and pleasures as a gift to be enjoyed. He also gave us boundaries to protect that gift, boundaries to ensure maximum enjoyment and freedom, and boundaries that prevent guilt, shame, regret, and ultimately the destruction of that gift. When the boundary of sexual purity before marriage is disregarded and violated, the enjoyment of His gift is lessened and corrupted. Persistent violation of those safe perimeters will eventually replace all enjoyment with shame and fear. Many couples get married only to discover one or both of them is broken in the area of enjoyment due to the violation of boundaries in the past. God, in His grace and mercy, can mend the broken pieces, but…oh, the joy of having no broken pieces to begin with!

Maybe your parents have a marriage that you admire and desire for yourself; but maybe they don't. If they are working through their past mistakes and are making a go of it, I'd say their efforts are admirable, to say the least; I wish more couples had that fortitude. But don't take their example, however good or bad, and aim for the same. Aim for higher, better, purer, and more glorious examples! Make a decision within yourself to stay pure for the spouse God is preparing for you. There are some folks who need a list of rules; but the highest standard flows out of a sincere love for God. He will show you by His Spirit and with your own conscience when to draw the line. Believe that it is worth it. Be a virgin at your marriage by choice.

GABE ON SAFEGUARDING YOUR COMPUTER

In a general homeschool environment where the kids know way more about the computer than you do, you (not the kid next door, or your smartest kid, YOU) need to take control and educate yourself. Pornography of the vilest sort will literally be looking for your kids; perverts (ages 9 to 99, believe me…) with completely destructive intent will be trolling the chat-rooms for the naïve. There is no reason for a child who is not yet worldly wise to even have the opportunity to encounter these things. Make them worldly wise on your own terms in your own time. Now let me give you some basic suggestions:

Q: How can I control the internet in my home?

A: The best way to control the internet in your home is to have a password system that allows only the one who knows the password to access the internet. You also have to understand that there is more than one password that you should be aware of. If you have an internet connection, there is already an existing password that allows you to log in to your internet account. That is NOT the password I am talking about. The password you need will allow or disallow internet access of any type on your computer.

To learn how to set up a password for internet permissions with step-by-step instructions, go to:

nogreaterjoy.org/index.php?id=control-your-net

This method will allow you to know about all access to the internet through your computer. Your children will have to come and ask you to type in the password so they can use the web. There will be no secret night-time web-surfing.

Q: If the password is discovered, how can I change to a new one?

A: The same place on your computer that allows you to

change user permissions will allow you to change the password for those permissions.

Q: Is it possible to check which web sites were visited during someone's use of the internet?

A: Yes. You can check the "history" in your "internet browser" by opening your internet service and typing Control-H (pressing the "control" key and the "H" key simultaneously). The recent history of your internet viewing will appear when you type Control-H. Most people, however, who have any computer savvy will be able to erase their tracks. So don't depend on this alone. Watching and being aware is the surest method.

Q: I've heard about internet filters or filtered internet. How good are they? How can I get one?

A: First of all, filters don't work that well; some pornography will still get through. Let's say this: if your filter promises to keep out 99.99% of all porn, and there are a million sites with some pornography on them, then you still have 10,000 porn pages that can get through to you. In many cases, it's good that you cut out so much, but you can't really depend on the filter to keep porn out of your computer.

Secondly, most internet filters also cut out a lot of internet information that doesn't have anything to do with pornography. For instance, if you want to check out a news page and there is some reference to sex on the page, you may not be able to access the news. Some of those instances of information might be well worth living without. You make that decision. However, I believe that learning to live knowledgeably in a highly technical society will be necessary for most of your kids.

If you decide you need a filter, the best one I've run across is surfcontrol.com. There are also filtered internet services that are often advertised in Christian magazines.

I believe that the problem with porn and other deviant content on the web is not insurmountable. We do need people to help in the fight.

BEKA ON SAFEGUARDING YOUR CIRCUMSTANCES:

I suggest buying a glass door for the computer room. This will shut out the sound for those who need to study in silence, but allow for constant observation and accountability. The doors on the offices of No Greater Joy Ministries are glass. No one is allowed to have secrets. You might also consider moving the computer room to a highly trafficked area where people are walking by continually.

Dad built our house so that all the bedroom doors face the main living room/family room. None of our doors had locks on them until we were older, and then only the girls. We were never allowed to spend time in our rooms behind closed doors. The door could only be closed for five minutes of clothes changing. If a door was closed for a longer period of time, Dad was likely to walk in unannounced to see what we were up to.

The next step to safeguarding your family is to teach them how to react WHEN (not if) they encounter immorality. Here is a short list of topics to discuss:

- What to do when they find pornography on the computer, or in a magazine.
- What to do when a friend or relative shows them something vile.
- What to say when evil suggestions or comments are made.
- What to do when someone tries to molest them.
- What to do with evil thoughts and imaginations.

In our quiet, little Amish community where kids are shel-
tered like nowhere else, one day there came a family who had
been "around the block", with each other, with their neighbors, and their pets. Very gross things! They dressed Amish
and talked the talk. But one day, soon after they came, their
ten-year-old son was playing with the other boys after church
service. He offered to tell the boys how to copulate with a dog.
One of the boys in that crowd had been raised by a daddy who
had prepared him for such an assault. The young boy refused
to listen and walked away to tell on the kid who was offering his perverse information. The family, who hung around for
money and other hopeful evils, was asked to stay away from
our church and community. This safety for the whole Church
was provided by one daddy who told his son how to react in
such an ungodly situation.

Another precaution my parents took was to limit—almost
to nothing—our staying overnight with cousins or best friends.
Now, as a mother myself, I plan to eliminate that possibility
altogether for my children. Even the most conservative friends
and cousins of mine had told me things I shouldn't have heard
as a kid. Now that I'm grown, I'm amazed to look back and find
out that most of the few girls who spent the night with me once
in a blue moon had been molested, even during the very years I
knew them. Once they grew up, they told on the criminals who
molested them. Back then, they were silent through fear and
were ignorant of the evil things that were happening to them.

The statistics of child molestation in America are horren-
dous. One out of every two girls is messed with, and one out
of every four boys. Our pastor's wife out here in Gallup, New
Mexico, made sure her daughter stayed in the bedroom with
them every time they had company. Even if the company was

family! She didn't trust her own brothers and cousins around her daughter. She was wise. Her daughter is now grown and free of any grief of that sort. The mother herself wasn't so protected as a child.

There are so many stories I could tell of the despicable boldness of a molester who harmed a child, even when the house—and even the room—was full of people. Never let your little children sit on the lap of someone you are not absolutely sure of. And never be so sure as to fail to pay attention to what is going on. Make sure your little girls wear tights, under shorts, or pantaloons of some kind that make access to their private parts difficult, and make modesty easier. Don't just close your eyes and hope they make it to adulthood safely. They won't if you don't fight for them. The Bible says, "watch and pray." Praying for them must be accompanied by attentive "watching" for their souls and their safety.

The last, but not least, precaution I would recommend is to assure your children of God's hatred for those who sexually harm children. My dad read to us the scriptures about God's judgment on those who "offend one of these little ones", and told us plainly what actions would be categorized as an offense. He described God breaking the arms (Psalm 10:15), and bashing in the teeth (Psalm 3:6; 58:6) of the men who rape little girls. He talked about them burning in the lake of fire for eternity. I was so convinced of God's hatred for child molesters, I even felt sorry for them. If someone had ever molested me, it would not have crossed my mind to remain silent, because I would have been so positive that I was being wronged, and that they were doing something evil to me. So many molesters put a guilt trip on the children and convince them that they are just being "loved." I knew without one doubt that molestation wasn't love. Assure your children of God's righteous judgment on those who harm children, and enlist them to help you watch out for those evil people.

SCRIPTURE PASSAGES AND TOPICS TO READ WITH YOUR CHILDREN:

Holy Sex:
> Gen. 1:28; Prov. 18:22; Job 31:1; Pro. 5:15-19; Gen. 26:8; Eph 5:31; Heb. 13:4; Song of Solomon; Prov. 30:18-19

Healthy Relationships with the Opposite Sex:
> 1 Cor. 7:1-9; 1Tim. 5:2

The Figure of Christ and the Bride:
> Ezek. 16:8; Isa. 54:5; Eph. 5; Isa. 62:5

Sodomy:
> Lev. 18:22; Gen. 19; Lev. 20:13; Deut. 23:17; 1 Kings 14:24; Rom. 1:26-27

Child Molestation:
> Matt. 18:5-10

Bestiality:
> Lev. 18:23; Exod. 22:19; Deut. 27:21; Lev. 20:15-16

Incest:
> Lev. 20:17-21

Fornication:
> Prov. 5:20-23; Prov. 6:24-35; Prov. 7; 1 Thess. 4:3; 1 Cor. 6:18

Uncleanness:
> Matt. 5:28; 1 Cor. 6:13-20; 1 Cor. 6:9; 1 Tim. 1:9-10

Speaking of Things Done in Darkness:
> Eph. 5:3-7; 5:12; Prov. 5:3-5; Prov. 2:11-20

**ASK YOUR CHILDREN THESE QUESTIONS AND
PROVOKE A DISCUSSION.**

What are these things?

Who does them?

What is the penalty for these sins?

What did God do to the nations that practiced
these things?

What will He do to the individual offender?

This should not be a one-time discussion. Let the information flow as naturally as possible. Let there be an openness in your conversation that will give your children confidence to continue to ask questions. Dad did not call a "church" meeting when he discussed these things. It was "a little here and a little there," in the context of daily life. If we saw a broken individual, or read something in the paper, or heard a friend discussing a sad situation, Dad would speak of the sin, what the Bible said, and how the sin had caused such pain. He did not hide the gossip of sin from us; he used it as an illustration of good and evil. He made the concept of sowing and reaping part of our daily communication; evil brings judgment and death; righteousness brings reward and life.

Look into your children's eyes when you speak of these ugly sins. Read their souls. Some of you will be shocked. If you gain their trust, in time you may receive some heart-breaking news. Your children will at last be emboldened to confess wrongs they have done or had done to them. Be prepared to minister to them with love and compassion. Be equipped with the gospel of Jesus Christ, which will cleanse them from the stains of sin that have been burdening them. Be prepared to weep with your children, and begin a process of healing. Your heart will break, and I have no consolation for you except that you now can prevent further harm, and can minister to your children while there is yet hope for their recovery.

To the rest of you, rejoice, and walk circumspectly! You are saving the next generation from a crippling evil, which Satan is using to enslave boys and girls and men and women, to the destruction of families and nations. God will bless you for preserving your boys and girls, enabling them to someday come together in fantastic marriages and strong families. God has placed their future in your hands. Read back through these materials regularly, studying the verses listed and the suggestions given. Prayerfully embark on a sure course that demonstrates your commitment to protect your children from this hideous, Satanic attack on the children. Finally, "The grace of the Lord Jesus Christ, and the love of God, and the communion of the Holy Spirit, be with you all. Amen."

Created to be His Help Meet

What God is doing through this book is amazing. Has it provoked you to want to be the help meet God created you to be? We pray so. If it has blessed you (and your beloved) then consider passing the blessing on to someone you love by purchasing *Created to be His Help Meet* for them. *Available in: single volumes, cases of 24 (40% discount) and audio reading CDs.* Available in English or Spanish.

Help Meet's Journey

The Journey is a year-long companion journal for Created to be His Help Meet, in which you can create a lasting memory of the miracle God is doing in you. This workbook includes 123 pages of studies and diary pages, plus extra pages for stories, memory-making, recipes, doodling, and pictures. This is a perfect study guide both for individuals and for women's study groups. 123-pg. Journal • Available in single volumes or case quantity of 24.

Marriage God's Way Video

A perfect marriage is 100/100. It is a man and a woman giving 100% to the other. What if he or she won't give 100%? Then you can match their 10% with your 10% and continue in an unfulfilling relationship, or, by the grace of God and the power of the Holy Spirit, you can give 100% to your spouse for their sake and watch their 10% grow into 100%.

Michael takes the viewer through the Word of God to uncover the Divine plan for husbands and wives. Available on 2 DVDs.

Only Men

Michael Pearl speaks directly and frankly to men about their responsibilities as husbands. Wives should not listen to this tape. We don't want you taking advantage of your man. Available on 1 CD or 1 Cassette.

Holy Sex

Michael Pearl takes his readers through a refreshing journey of Biblical texts, centered in the Song of Solomon. This sanctifying look at the most powerful passion God ever created will free the reader from false guilt and inhibition. Michael Pearl says, "It is time for Christian couples to take back this sacred ground and enjoy the holy gift of sexual pleasure." 82 page Book.

To Train Up a Child - 500,000+ In Print! -

From successful parents, learn how to train up your children rather than discipline them up. With humor and real-life examples, this book shows you how to train your children before the need to discipline arises. Be done with corrective discipline; make them allies rather than adversaries. The stress will be gone and your obedient children will praise you. 122 page Book.

The Joy of Training

Michael and Debi Pearl tell how they successfully trained up their five children with love, humor, the rod, and a King James Bible. The 2 DVD set contains the same high quality, digitally filmed content as the video set and hundreds of snapshots and video clips of family and children, illustrating the things being taught. Available on DVD.

Sin No More

The big question is: "So how do I stop sinning?" You have confessed your sins, received the baptism of the Holy Ghost with evidence of everything but ceasing to sin, yet you are still a Romans 7 defeated Christian. I assure you, God not only saves his children from the penalty of sin but he saves them from its power as well. You can stop sinning. Available in a 9 CD set, 1 MP3 CD or 7 Cassette set.

Good and Evil

Written by Michael Pearl and featuring spectacular artwork by Marvel Comic artist Danny Bulanadi. Over 300 pages illustrated in comic book format show the Bible stories in a chronological approach. Great for any child, teen or as Sunday School material. 312 page Book.

Righteousness

This set contains four messages on salvation and righteousness: The Man Christ Jesus, Saving Righteousness, Imputed Righteousness, and The Blood. The messages explore intriguing topics such as the humanity of Christ and why he referred to himself as "The Son of Man", why man's blood is required when he spills the blood of another man, God's clearly defined method of making a person righteous enough to get to heaven, and how the blood of Jesus washes away our sins. Available in a 4 CD set.

Teaching Responsibility

The difference between a man and a boy, no matter how old, is his willingness to bear his responsibility. In this seminar, Michael Pearl uses humorous stories and practical examples to illustrate the simple process of training your children to work without complaint. Cut into his speaking presentation are hundreds of video clips and photos that help illustrate his message. 2 DVD set.

Eight Kingdoms

The Bible speaks of eight kingdoms. You can't see one of them. One is coming but you can't be a part of it. Another must be resisted. You have been removed from another. You must honor another that is evil. One is now fighting for its life. One is going to smash all the others and reign forever on the earth. If you don't want to be challenged, don't bother buying this book. This book would be a gift your pastor would truly enjoy.